THE WAITING ROOM

BY:
CARRIE GEORGE

Dedication

To Mom and Daddy, you have always encouraged me with your love and your strong faith. Your positive outlook that God will take care of things has influenced my life forever.

Prologue

Life has a way of teaching us things we don't always want to know. For me, I was to learn that there is much value to be found in and through the process of waiting. But what I didn't know was that I would be in literally dozens of hospital waiting rooms over a time span of seventeen years. It has been a difficult lesson, for there are many components to the art of waiting that have taken years to learn. Although many of these stories have evolved from literal waiting rooms, a few have been written from a metaphorical sense: a waiting room in which we inevitably find ourselves at one time or another.

The stories you are about to read are true. Each one was carefully and deliberately penned with the hope of touching your heart in an encouraging way. By reading these stories you may identify with one of the characters, or relate to a similar circumstance as you recall a time sitting in your own waiting room. It is in this very place, our personal waiting room, where life's comedies, dramas, tragedies, and unsolved mysteries seem to unfold in a unique pattern of timing and sequencing of events. Our family's journey has caused me to grow in my relationship with God, and I have discovered Him in places I had not seen Him before. I realize now that He was with us, walking close by our sides through every trial. He is with you along your journey as well.

The Characters

Jeff ~ My husband of twenty-three years, boyfriend for life. I met Jeff one month after giving my heart to Jesus. What an incredible gift he's been to my entire family and me! His handsome looks and slender, athletic frame conceal the health adversities he has faced over the years. Jeff donated his kidney to our son Kevin, but the transplant was rejected and removed within the week. Jeff has been a tower of strength, comfort, and wisdom as he guided our family through heartbreak, disappointment and discouragement. He has mentored me since the day we met twenty six years ago, modeling the gift of wisdom and integrity in ways that I someday hope to emulate. I am proud to be his wife and confidant, but most of all, to be the love of his life.

Jason ~ He is my firstborn son and soul mate from a previous marriage and is now twenty nine years old. Jason and I share a unique bond and deep relationship, which has only grown stronger through the trials and tears during his teenage years of rebellion. At the age of twenty-four, Jason returned to school and finished his high school education and was rewarded with a graduation ceremony that brought our entire family together, including his father, stepmother, half brothers and sister. I joke with Jason and tell him that he has taught me everything I never wanted to know. Faced with his purple hair, a pierced nose, and tattooed body, I learned to look deeper than what appeared on the surface. I discovered that it is in a sacred place that hidden treasures are tucked away... in the heart of one's soul. As a result, deep truths are carved in me forever.

I will never judge a person by their looks again, for I have learned without a doubt that one's outer appearance does not reflect the heart inside.

Kevin ~ Nicknamed "Kevin from Heaven," he truly has been a precious gift to us all. Kevin's birth announced the beginning of new things. He was born with a rare condition and, due to its severity, required surgery by his first birthday. This would be the first of several unsuccessful operations, including a failed kidney transplant at the age of two. To date, Kevin is now eighteen years old and has undergone fourteen surgeries, including a second kidney transplant. This kidney is still working well after fourteen years. Someday, when it becomes necessary to be placed on the donor list once again, Kevin will face his own waiting room experience. Perhaps with the history of his own story, he will discover that he has learned the art very well. After all, the preparation for waiting began the day he was born.

Other Characters

Lewis, Mary, Juan (name changed), Alex, Dr. Bunny, Dr. Nelson, Derek, Glen, Rebecca, Pastor Rick, Nick, Anthony and Shelley's stories appear in this book also. They are fellow patients, doctors, and friends.

Acknowledgements

To Jeff, the husband of my heart... Your love gives me strength. Thank you for your constant support, quiet encouragement and practical wisdom which have anchored me through many storms. My heart still beats wildly for you.

To my precious sons, Jason and Kevin... You both have shown me how to live with courage, taught me how to pray, and always to hope for the best; the greatest gifts a mother could ask for. My love for you goes beyond words.

To Marzia, my daughter in law...You are a perfect fit in our family, and an amazing gift to our son..

To Julie...Because of your vision and gift of encouragement, this book has been written. Thank you for the coaching meetings and rich prayer times, assuring me that these stories needed to be shared.

To the women from Tuesday Morning Bible Study...the work that God has done in our hearts have knitted us together forever.

To Pastors Zac and Julie, Bill and Anjje, Rick and Susie, Byron and Lynda, Jon and Shannon, and the Salt Lake Christian Fellowship Prayer Chain...your prayers, wisdom and grace keep our family on God's path of love. How can we ever thank you enough?

To all our family and friends, especially Ron and Mary, Wayne and Jan, George and Leisa, Geneva, Cricket, and Janie....supporting us with your love and prayers is the glue which held us together. May God's grace and love be returned to you a hundredfold.

Table of Contents

1

Introduction to the Waiting Room

Years of failed surgeries, disappointment, and despair paved the way for this book to be written. For more than ten years, our lives were in a cycle of crisis, trauma, and grief. A desperate plea from the deepest place of my heart welled up, "Lord, please send us a miracle." I longed to be released from this prison of captivity, where I was shackled to fear and anxiety, running on adrenaline instead of peace and fighting the night terror of taunting dreams.

From the backdrop of trials and darkness, a flickering light of hope began to emerge. New thoughts gave birth to a dawn of acceptance, illuminating higher insights to a mind once darkened with doubt. Faith replaced fear and an inner peace infused my being, allowing me to accept the course ahead.

But it was in this dark place, the waiting room, where my Lord, through His Word, became my strong tower, refuge, and strength. I came to the end of myself, and found instead a hiding place in the shadow of His wings. I share this book with the hope that you too will find Him in your own way, in your own time of need.

At one time or another, we are all in this place - *the waiting room*. Over the years, I have learned that waiting is not so much about where it will take me, but rather how I would respond to it. When I embraced the vision of *the waiting room* as a special place to grow, designed uniquely for my needs, it became a special retreat, a secret place where my thoughts would be tested and tried by His Word and through prayer.

The journey of faith and the road of trials help us to become more like Christ. As I accepted our course, and surrendered to the journey, beautiful things began to spring forth from my soul

Our destiny had been charted
Our course was set.
This would be a journey
Across unchartered territory
For our family…one which
Required faith, perseverance, hope,
And prayer.
Never give up!

Sing Songs of Praise When Your Heart Is Weary

2

Rocking and Waiting

*J*eff and I hurried to the Waiting Room the moment he left our side. The operating room was just beyond those doors, the doors which separated us from the many questions which would arise over the next several hours. We waited all day, along with dozens of other parents who would jump to their feet when their names were called. They would take the phone call from the surgical nurse, pack up their reading materials, and then leave.

We waited for our turn, but the phone did not ring for us. Two hours passed, and a knot began to form in my stomach. Timidly walking up to the lady behind the desk, I asked if she would please check and see if our son had left the operating room. During Kevin's office visit, the surgeon told us the operation would take just a little over an hour. She reported to us that Kevin was still in surgery. Thinking they must have begun late, we settled back into our seats, staring blindly at more magazines, and waited. Another two hour passed; something had to be wrong!

After what seemed like an eternity, the phone finally rang for us. Seven long and anxious hours of waiting finally came to an end. The surgeon came and spoke with us, assuring us that things went well, but he had discovered more work needed to be done than originally anticipated. He said it would be fine for us to go back and see our son in recovery.

Jeff and I were not prepared for the sight we saw. Kevin's body was twice his normal size! Swollen with fluids, he looked like the Pillsbury dough boy. When he woke up, the first thing he wanted to do was to put his thumb in his mouth. But because of the I.V. which was taped to a straight board in his hand, it wouldn't reach. He started to cry, and so did I. I could not bear seeing my little boy in this condition.

Over the next few days, we tried consoling him, but nothing seemed to help. No matter what position I held him in, he could not seem to get comfortable and cried most of the time. Four nights later, tired, discouraged, and emotionally drained, I was holding him in the rocking chair, wondering if he would ever settle down and go to sleep. So far, he had only slept for fifteen to thirty minute intervals, after which he would wake up crying again.

Suddenly, as soft as a gentle breeze, I heard a quiet voice deep inside my heart. It whispered: "Sing praises to me." There was such an exquisite peace that came with that message, I could not ignore it. Way down past the pain and heartache, a song emerged from within. Softly but audibly, in the pediatric unit at two o'clock in the morning, I began to sing. And the more I sang, the stronger my spirit grew. I felt like I was being washed in a divine bubble bath of peace. I just had to keep singing to keep it flowing. Tears rolled down my cheeks as I looked down and saw my Kevin had finally fallen asleep. His body had relaxed for the first time in days, and so did mine.

Many times, I have looked back on that night when I was at my weakest and remembered the powerful impact praise had on my spirit. It has reminded me in other challenging situations to lift my voice in song and praise. Each time, the effect of his peace has settled the instability of my emotions. It's amazing how the Lord inhabits our praises. This was a lesson I personally could only learn while sitting in a rocking chair, praising Him in and through a difficult circumstance. Not for the sake of moving my lips…but for the sake of Him moving my heart.

Acts 16:25 "About midnight Paul and Silas were praying and singing hymns to God and the other prisoners were listening to them." When you're in difficult circumstances, there's something to be said about singing praises to God in the wee hours of the morning. When Paul and Silas started to sing, the doors flew open, and prisoner's chains came loose. And when we sing, the door of peace flies open and looses us from chains of fear.

3

An Inner Preparation Begins

*B*elow is an excerpt from my prayer journal, dated 11/25/87. When I wrote this, I did not know that what lie in wait was the deepest valley, the darkest shadow and the steepest mountain our family would ever climb. I write this today, sixteen years later, for it has taken that long to be able to process these thoughts without the acute presence of pain. I have emerged from these trying times with a quiet, strong, and steadfast faith and a greater understanding of His love. I could not have known Him so intimately and passionately without first sharing in this fellowship of suffering.

"As an encouragement to myself I shall write what I feel in my spirit deep within me, which is contrary to what I feel as a person. Deep within my soul, my God tells me He's chosen me, long ago, to be a special servant for Him. He tells me that from every difficult trial, I learn more and more the virtues of my Creator and I must trust in Him; not the circumstances. Through the trials, I come closer to the Lord God even when I am angry with Him. He understands and has compassion beyond my comprehension. He says He's in control, don't be dismayed. He is doing a great work within me, my husband, and my family. I submit to Him, for I am lost without His loving comfort. Help me, Lord. Amen.

"For just as the sufferings of Christ are ours in abundance, so also our comfort is abundant through Christ." (2Cor. 1:5)

Learning To Know Christ Through the Fellowship of Suffering

Philippians 3:10

4

The Surgery That Rocked our World

*J*uly 12, 1988. On that day, we were met by the kidney transplant team, a group of three surgeons, who would remove my husband's right kidney and transplant it into our son. Last minute details were discussed, a flurry of activity began, and the seemingly oversized gurney arrived too soon for our two and a half year old son.

There we were, stepping onto the elevator, descending from the children's wing on the fifth floor to the surgical ward two floors below. Kevin's thumb instinctively found its way to his mouth and he lay there sucking it hungrily. His other little arm was taped to a small white board which supported the I.V. in his little arm. Standing beside the large bed on wheels, we both felt the anxiety rise as the elevator took us down.

The doors opened, and the nurses hesitated so we could lean over and kiss our boy once more. There are no words to describe the anguish a parent feels as their child is wheeled away to a destiny over which they have no control. As she rolled him away from us, I could feel myself straining towards those double doors which rocked back and forth until they finally closed, wanting to snatch him into my arms and flee from this place. Just then, I was startled from my reverie by the nurse calling Jeff's name. A knot of apprehension formed in my belly while I watched him climb onto the gurney awaiting him. I remember swallowing hard to fight back the tears. I never felt so all alone. Having both my husband and my son in surgery at the same time was the most unnatural feeling in the world. Jason was gone, too. He was out in California spending time with his father and stepmother and their family. I needed Jeff with me that day, telling me everything would be alright. How would I face hours of waiting without his comforting presence and strength by my side?

As the surgery doors closed once more, I was suddenly aware of the vast, empty hallway looming in front of me. This was a strange day, full of hope yet ridden with fear. Intuitively, I made my way towards the waiting room, whispering prayers for safety and protection over my husband and my son. The waiting room was filled with well wishers from church, and the long wait began.

Hours later, the elevator doors opened and Pastor Bill leapt to his feet as he caught a glimpse of Jeff's gurney being wheeled down the hallway. He grabbed me by the hand and said: "Hey, you want to go see your husband?" His enthusiasm caught me by surprise and we had to run to catch up with them. When we did, I carefully leaned over and kissed Jeff's pale, colorless face. Groggily he teased, "That was the most fun I've ever had. Whose idea was this anyway?" His words were music to my ears! Pastor Bill looked like the proud papa and chuckled at Jeff's attempt at humor.

Our family gained popularity throughout the hospital as the story of the successful transplant circulated among the staff. I would ride the elevator to the fifth floor to visit Jeff, only to be greeted by a hand-made sign sitting on his pillow which read, "Gone to visit my kidney." Smiling, I would ride the elevator back down to the third floor and find my two favorite patients grinning back at me with eyes revealing their secret bond, Jeff's organ now living inside our son.

Kevin absolutely glowed; he looked so healthy and pink and seemed to be responding well to the transplant. Day four exuberantly announced continued success and the following day Jeff was sent home to continue his recuperation. This was a textbook transplant all the way through, until the evening of the fifth day post transplant.

I was now about to enter a new classroom of waiting, a student of life's harder lessons, learning to trust and accept God's answer when everything seems to fall apart.

Utter Mayhem
Aligns
My Path to
Sweet Surrender

5

Two Words

*E*xploratory surgery revealed that half the kidney had already turned black, just five days post transplant. It was decided that a powerful drug would be administered to Kevin in hopes of saving the kidney. The joy ride was over. Somber faces encircled my baby's crib and doctors and nurses whispered passionately regarding their next approach. Kevin was suddenly very sick and his little body lay unnaturally still.

Apparently, by this point, I had gone into shock and the doctor called my friends Ron and Mary to come and bring me home. They assured me they would do everything possible and that I would not be able to see Kevin for the rest of that night. Everything seemed surreal. Life seemed to go into slow motion, and I felt like I was drifting along in a fog bank. I barely remember the ride home as Mary drove my car.

Entering our home that night, I was struck by the quiet darkness in contrast to the bright lights and many voices back at the hospital. Jeff was lying in bed as he had been released from the hospital just the day before to continue recuperating from surgery. A very concerned look shadowed his face when he saw me; instinct told him something was wrong.

Before I could even explain why I was home, loud noises erupted from somewhere outside. Mary was still downstairs, so she was the first one to open the front door and discover that her husband, Ron, was on the ground struggling against a woman and her husband who were pounding on him with their fists. Jeff hobbled down the stairs to see what the commotion was all about. Our next door neighbor hurried over with a gun, offering protection and shouting at the couple to get off of Ron. Security showed up as sheer pandemonium broke loose on our front lawn. Still in shock, I wandered around, my eyes taking in what was going on but my mind not comprehending it.

Eventually things settled down and the couple was escorted away. Ron began to explain to the Security Officer what had happened so he could fill out a report. While Ron was driving behind Mary and me, he had made a sudden lane change in front of this couple's car. This angered them, so they tailgated Ron all the way up to our driveway, speeding past the Security Guard who then jumped in his patrol vehicle to chase them down. When Ron got out of his car, they jumped him from behind and started screaming at him and hitting him while he was on the ground.

It was utter mayhem at our house while my son lay in a hospital crib, fighting for his life. I was grateful for the desensitizing effect shock temporarily numbed me with, but it only lasted for the night. By dawn, I was fully aware of the gnawing pain eating at me. There are times when God seems far away, and this surely was one of them.

Early the next morning, the hospital called requesting that we come immediately. We learned that Kevin had nearly died the night before, and the doctors wanted our decision as they explained the two options left. The surgeons wanted to remove the kidney, but the nephrology team wanted to try another dose of a powerful anti rejection drug; which could save the transplant but could also prove fatal. There clearly was strong disagreement as to what should be done. They needed our decision within thirty minutes.

We walked out of the surgical ward and found our pastor and his wife waiting for us. To this day I do not know how they knew to be there at such a critical time, and we were grateful for their presence. After talking it over with them, we slipped away to pray in the hospital chapel. My husband was the rock and the stabilizer at the time. His heart told him the answer the moment he closed his eyes. We found the team of doctors waiting for us, and Jeff gave them our final decision. The kidney was removed and a permanent catheter was inserted into his peritoneum for life on dialysis. I remember walking in a daze towards the exit doors, completely depleted of faith. I was angry and I screamed at God because I couldn't see His plan for good. "And we know that in all things God works for the good of those who love him, who have been called according to his purpose." (Rom. 8:28)

But we don't always see things clearly at the time when we are in the midst of the circumstance. I found so many scripture verses which spoke to this evening, like Psalm 121:7-8 for example. "The Lord will keep you from all harm, he will watch over your life; the Lord will watch over your coming and going both now and forevermore."

That night, as I look back on things and recognize the blessing of his peace and his presence which came to me in the form of my body's reaction to shock; somehow deep inside my spirit there continued to be a message of hope. A message that his character was being formed in us. He was preparing us for a journey that would bring glory to His Name.

I now look at this verse from Philippians 3:10 with fondness, as it has brought greater revelation to my own heart: "I want to know Christ and the power of his resurrection and the fellowship of sharing in his sufferings, becoming like him in his death." I did not know where all this was heading, but I knew in my heart my God loved us and He had a plan. I stopped asking "why" and began to ask Him to ***change me***. Healing began as I learned the gentle path of surrender.

6

The Spirit Never Slumbers

On the seventh day of the kidney transplant, the failed organ was removed from Kevin's body. As though his little body knew no other coping mechanism, our son fell into a very deep sleep. For six days we wondered if he would ever awaken, and then worried what new problem might develop once he did.

Would he be the same? Would those beautiful blue eyes still look at me with full comprehension? Would his sweet little voice still mimic his grown up style of speaking?

As time passed, we felt that the coma had been a blessing of protection, shielding his frail little body from further trauma. Several months later, we were amazed to discover the powerful way the spirit had been at work while his body slumbered.

7

Coma Courage

Often, we find that the course of pain we travel leads us to the destination of insight. Although its path is wearisome, clouded by doubt and uncertainties, we can always trust that at the end, comes light. The darkness is dispelled by light, confusion is cleared by truth, and sorrow is replaced by joy. We feel compelled to draw inwardly as the journey towards revelation becomes painful, but the response of a surrendered soul wins the victory, gains understanding, and settles in peace. One such course was during a six day period of silence.

His tiny, beautiful body lay perfectly still under the white covers of the hospital crib bed. Wires and tubes hung from various machines, reaching into his arms and chest, as though offering their support at his time of need. He had not moved for six days, nor even opened his eyes. Kevin was only two and a half years old at the time, much too young to have endured such an ordeal.

Standing by his crib in the ICU for hours on end, caressing his plentiful brown hair, kissing his pale, innocent cheek, I remember reading a small book called <u>Hinds Feet on High Places.</u> This book seemed to bring comfort as I related to the main character, "Much Afraid." Each day brought more questions than answers, more challenges than I had faith.

Kevin's first few words had been the typical Momma, Dadda…but then one day he floored us with: "Pizza!" He was less than a year old and finding ways to communicate his unusual maturity to us. Our friends were amused by his grown up speech; they said it was like talking to a miniature adult. As I stood next to his bed now, I wondered if my little man who articulated so clearly would ever speak again.

Periodically, I would glance over my book which I held in one hand while gently touching his limp form with the other. Before turning the next page I would stop reading and look to see if any change had taken place in his face. I would sing my little made up song to him…"Mommy loves you, daddy loves you, Jason loves you, Jesus loves you!" For some reason, I always felt better after singing it to him. A certain peace would settle over me then, and I hoped he felt it too.

The story in my book continued about how "Much Afraid" longed to follow the Good Shepherd up the steep, treacherous mountains, but her lameness prevented her from traveling too far. Maybe my legs worked fine, but I sure was having a hard time climbing this hill of worry. Much Afraid also wanted to feel love, but the Good Shepherd explained to her that it would require her to agree to receive a thorn of pain in her heart. I couldn't remember asking my Good Shepherd for such a gift, but certainly the thorn had strategically and carefully been placed deep into my mother's heart. Much Afraid decided, after considering the implication of grief she would endure, that the love she sought after and dreamed of was worth the cost, and so she accepted it. Immediately, the prick of that thorn produced its two fold purpose, pain and love. It was deep, immeasurable love, the kind she had hoped for her whole life. To assist her on her new journey, the Good Shepherd sent her two companions. Their names were Grace and Joy. Gaining courage as I read on, I sensed the Good Shepherd's question for me: Would I accept the thorn of this path He had chosen for me?

A few days later, my sister Deanna and cousin Dana flew in from California to come visit my sleeping son. Laying their hands on his still frame, they prayed and cried and asked the Lord to let him awaken again. We then left for lunch, and when we came back, Kevin's body was still in the same position. Wanting to feel him close to me, I scooped him up into my arms and rocked him while singing my little song to him.

Without warning, his eyes suddenly opened, looked straight into mine, and asked in his most charming voice, "Mommy, can I get back in bed now?" Amazed by this sudden change and over-whelmed with joy, I laughed and cried and laughed some more. A miracle had happened. My Good Shepherd had awakened my child by sending me two companions too!

It was a slow recovery, and Kevin would not be allowed to go home for another month. But when he did, he found our street lined with balloons, posters, and a new swing set from Grammie and Paparon waiting for him in our back yard. His brother Jason gently pushed him on the swing, careful to not let it climb too high. Squeals of delight filled the air and it was a happy homecoming, but also bittersweet, since that thorn brought a new pain into our life; he would now go to sleep attached to a dialysis machine.

Two months later, as Kevin's favorite stuffed animals and Bert and Ernie's smiling faces looked down on him from his bookshelf, I tucked my precious boy in for the night. The machine had been hooked up to the catheter in his tummy, and I leaned over to kiss him good night. "Mommy?" Kevin smiled. "Mommy loves me, Daddy loves me, Jason loves me, and Jesus loves me!"

He heard. He really had heard my song! Not even a coma could shut out the voice of love from this mother's heart to her son.

"I prayed to the Lord and he answered me, freeing me from all my fears. Those who look to him for help will be radiant with joy" (Psalm 34:4-5)

An earthly angel
Responds
To a heavenly
Prayer

How God can answer a mother's
deepest plea through
strangers unaware....

8

An Angel Named Lewis

The doctors strongly encouraged us to go home at night and get some rest. Since Kevin would be in here for a month, it was best for all of us if we would go home at night and take a break. They wanted us to be fresh in the morning; we would be trained over the next four weeks on how to perform dialysis at home. I understood their viewpoint and realized they were right, but I was his mother. Mothers don't leave their little ones in a hospital crib and then go home to sleep. I'm the one who bore this child, and now I found myself standing by his bed, just hoping for him to have a chance to enjoy his little, young life. It came so close to ending.

In a matter of days after the transplant, Kevin's body began to acutely reject the kidney that his father had donated to him. During the rejection process, an all-out effort was made to save the kidney, using a powerful drug. After administering this anti-rejection drug, Kevin almost died. His blood pressure dropped alarmingly low several times, but thanks to the heroic efforts of a young resident named Tom White, who was on the kidney transplant rotation at the time, Kevin's life was spared. Dr. White refused to leave his bedside until he was stabilized, even though he himself had not slept for over thirty-two hours.

Many sleepless nights came and went. I initially stayed at the hospital with Kevin, but eventually we followed their wise counsel and both of us went home to sleep late at night. The thirty minute drive home passed quickly in tired silence. In the car, I had prayed under my breath: "Lord, please send an angel to Kevin's room to stand by him and watch over him." Somehow, this prayer settled my anxiety and I felt a peaceful assurance, as though that prayer had alerted some angelic being to fly to my son's room and stand guard.

Several months after the failed transplant, we resumed the normal routine of attending church and fellowshipping with our friends. Jeff and I were standing around and talking with our friends at the end of the service one Sunday. As we told them how grateful we were to be home with our son again, a doctor who also was a member of our church came and joined our group. He was in research at the University Hospital and had visited us almost daily while Kevin was a patient there. He asked how his little friend was doing and went on to tell the group that Kevin had impacted many of the staff there, but, in particular, one young resident named Dr. Lewis. Intrigued, we listened to his account of the young doctor.

"Dr. Lewis heard about Kevin one night while he was on break in the doctor's lounge," he said. "Lewis worked the graveyard shift, and often the stories of morning surgical patients would trickle through the lounge late into the evening hours." "When he heard about Kevin, and the way he was described by some of his colleagues, he felt a tug in his heart to go see him."

"Dr. Lewis was a brand new Christian, so he didn't understand at the time that it was the work of the Holy Spirit pulling at his heart strings. When Lewis walked into Kevin's room at 3:00 a.m. that first time, he knew he was to pray over him." Our friend continued, "Dr. Lewis told me that he felt more peace after leaving his room than before entering it." "This became a nightly routine for him. Whenever he was on duty, he made sure he visited his little sleeping friend and would whisper a prayer for his full recovery."

As I listened to this tender story, I remembered my own prayer, several weeks before. Eyes brimming with tears, I thanked the Lord quietly for being so faithful – He indeed sent an angel to pray over my son while I was away. This angels' name was actually an earthly doctor...named Lewis.

After months of sleepless
nights,
A friend's heart
Is moved by
God's tender compassion...
Relieving this family's
Burden for a
Weekend to remember.

9

Modern Day Mary

John 15:13 says: "Greater love has no one than this that he lay down his life for his friends." This is a story about a friend who demonstrated this scripture, not by laying down her life to die, but by laying it down to live.

I was bone tired. After seven months of nightly dialysis and interrupted sleep, I finally reached my breaking point. I did not know how much longer I could cope. That day, I couldn't talk without tears rolling down my cheeks. I really needed a break, and I needed time alone with my husband. I wanted to have a normal conversation with him and not talk about hospitals, blood work, or dialysis solutions. I needed the assurance that I was still at the center of his heart as the woman he loved, that he would not just see me as a nurse and mother to our son. I also needed a block of sleep that was duty-free, without being awakened by the alarm from the dialysis machine.

I had always believed the adage that "God will never give you more than you can bear," but I was beginning to question those words. I felt drained, depleted of all reserve and there was no end in sight. As I was pouring out my heart to my friend Mary, she touched my arm to stop me, looked into my eyes, and said, "Train me to do the dialysis!" I didn't think she was serious; I thought she was just trying to make me feel better. After all, this was an enormous undertaking. It took Jeff and me several weeks at the hospital to learn to do this. Mary saw the disbelief on my face so she repeated her offer, "Train me to do the dialysis, and you and Jeff can go in your motor home and spend the weekend away." How can a friend be so unselfish and willing to take on such an enormous responsibility? At first, I refused her request and told her she was crazy. But as the days wore on, I felt myself toying with the idea of really having a weekend alone with my husband. I could feel myself becoming hopeful and light spirited again, just dreaming of a break and how it would refresh me.

After much discussion with Mary, Jeff, and our support nurses from the dialysis center, it was settled. The training with Mary began, and she appeared at our front door every night, right on time, to learn how to hook up Kevin to our resident dialysis machine, "Mr. Robot." Masks were donned, gloves snapped on, the work surface was disinfected, and Kevin's smile energized us as we prepared Mary for our weekend get away. Kevin really liked the idea of Aunt Mary learning to work with Mr. Robot and staying with him for a weekend. He was especially fond of my dearest friend, almost as if he sensed how close she was to my heart.

The day arrived for us to climb into our coach and drive away. It felt uncomfortable, very odd, and quite scary. Maybe I was wrong to take such a risk. What if something went wrong? What if the alarm went off so many times that poor Mary wouldn't get any sleep at all? Luckily, we would not be far from home since we had found a pleasant resort in a town only a short distance up the road. Even so, we still worried.

Jeff and I rolled into our camp site, pulled out the awning, set up the tables, and sat in the sun, soaking in the rays. This was heaven. We had been learning to trust God for the big things, but this was much smaller and yet more difficult in some ways learning to trust the Lord through the care of another's hands.

The frequent telephone calls and occasional worried thoughts could not erase the pleasure of being together. It was a weekend that gave profound relief.

At home, Mary slept lightly and prayed heavily. She was keenly aware of the seriousness of her responsibility and realized for the first time since the training started that Kevin's life was literally in her hands. She ended up journaling her experience over the weekend and how it impacted her, painting a clearer picture of our daily lives.

I came home refreshed and I was ready to resume my role as mother and caregiver once more. I like the way scripture can come to life at different times. In particular, "But only one thing is needed. Mary has chosen what is better and it will not be taken away from her." (Luke 10:42) This Mary had chosen to sit at the Lord's feet and listen.

He only needs to look down on the earth and find a heart that is ready to do whatever He asks. He looked down one day, and saw His servant-daughter, Mary. He saw that she too, had a listening heart...a heart that was ready to serve Him regardless of personal cost. His heart of compassion reached her own, as she turned her gaze upon our family. She agreed to be a vessel for His purposes, to touch a life in need. God has placed friends like these in your life, too. Are you allowing them the opportunity to serve God in your personal time of need?

We may not know
What tomorrow will bring,
But His Word assures us
That He is
Always there,
His plans
Are for our good.

10

A Future and a Hope

One morning I sat at our breakfast bar with my Bible open and feeling defeated. The kidney transplant from Dad had failed. Kevin would need to go through a transplant again, and in the meantime he needed time to heal and recover. Our nightly routine of putting our little toddler to bed, tucking him in and pulling up the covers had changed. Now, we had to scrub and disinfect the surface of a worktable, put on a mask and surgical gloves, and go through the procedure of connecting him to a dialysis machine.

This machine was quite large and impressive. We named the machine "Mr. Robot, as this is what it looked like to our son, Kevin. Kevin's favorite movie at the time was Short Circuit, so it seemed pretty cool to have his very own robot living in his room.

But the reality that Mr. Robot brought to our lives was the fact that he was doing the work of Kevin's kidneys, which were no longer in his body. Mr. Robot also had a way of waking us up several times during the night, as he would send off an alarm to let us know that the tubes were kinked, or the machine had malfunctioned during one of the cycles.

After several months of sleepless nights, we were exhausted. It was in this state that I sat at the breakfast bar, holding my head in my hands. Jason had already left for school on the bus, so I knew I was safe to let my guard down and just let my emotions come. I remember crying to the Lord, "Would it be this way forever?" I did not know what the future held, but we were told that small children could not live for long without receiving another transplanted kidney. This fact only added to my worries…would my sons grow up together?

Casually flipping the pages in my Bible, I noticed a passage I had not read before. Reading the words my eyes were drawn to, a sense of awe rose from within. It was almost as if the Lord had heard my question and now He was giving me His answer. "For I know the plans I have for you,' declares the Lord, plans to prosper you and not to harm you, to give you a future and a hope." (Jeremiah 29:11)

That morning, as the snow flurries covered the ground and the bare tree limbs received a soft, white blanket on its branches, I felt the Son of righteousness warm my heart with new hope. I didn't know the answer of what tomorrow would bring, but I knew that my Lord had answered the question of my heart…He would bring me good and not harm, and give me a future and a hope.

Blood Transfusion
Equals
Life Infusion
Life on Dialysis

11

Because Jesus Loves You

*K*evin was connected to a machine giving him a blood transfusion. We had learned so much about the function of the kidney and this was another sign that our son was truly relying on the help of modern medicine to keep him alive. In addition to nightly dialysis, every six weeks we would come to this section of the hospital and wait a few hours while he received a fresh transfusion of new red blood cells. As time slowly passed, my mind had plenty of opportunity to wander and revisit old stories, places, and people whose lives have touched us in some way. In light of the blood transfusion, one particular person came to mind, a little boy named Juan.

Juan was a nine year old AIDS patient who contracted this disease from a blood transfusion during surgery. A ministry I was involved with at the time in 1987, called B.J.L.Y. (Because Jesus Loves You) had taken on his case, to bring a last wish to this young boy's heart. My assignment was to arrange for his brother, Xavier, to come to the United States for the first time. Xavier lived in El Salvador and had not seen his brother Juan in seven years.

This seemed impossible to me, for there was great political unrest at that time in El Salvador, and I had never dealt with bureaucracy before. I didn't even like calling the phone company to straighten out a bill, let alone call the American Consulate in San Salvador. But the Lord knew I had a lot to learn about trusting Him and realizing how faithful He is. With butterflies in my stomach and trembling hands, I placed my first call to the Consulate of the United States Embassy in San Salvador. Explaining that I was calling from Manhattan Beach, I was about to give the nature of my call, when to my utter amazement, I hear the Ambassador of the American Consulate chuckle and say, "I'm from Manhattan Beach, too!" This connection immediately opened doors that only God Himself can do, and within five days, arrangements were made, a flight was donated, and papers came through to allow Xavier to leave his country.

As I stood at Los Angeles International Airport holding a sign with Xavier's name, I watched as this seventeen year old boy clear customs and then walk towards me, pointing at my sign. Somehow I remembered enough of my high school Spanish to communicate, and we were on our way in no time to bring these two brothers back together after a very long separation. Their years apart were quickly recovered in one long embrace. Little Juan had found comfort in the arms of his favorite brother. His wish had come true.

Many years later, as I sit here and watch my son receive one of many blood transfusions, I wonder how it is, knowing the risks involved with this procedure, that I am able to feel this peace wash over me as surely as the machine washes away the impurities from my little boy's body. As quickly as that thought came, another one immediately followed. It was as if my Lord was sitting right there with me and He seemed to say, "I saw you, when you held that boy with AIDS in your arms. His family was too afraid to go near him; they stood at the foot of his bed. But you sat down and embraced him in you arms; you gave him that hug that came from Me. My love is with you always, and my eyes are upon your child."

Who can explain the power of love? All I know is His love is ever present, and I'm learning to see Him everywhere. Are you?

As Christmas approached,
I discovered an early gift...
That His face was
more important
Than His hands.

12

His Face

Standing by the crackling fire, I warmed myself by the amber flames leaping up from the white-red logs. I had been thinking about the previous year when we had decorated our California home for Christmas with greenery and shiny colored balls. This year, in our new home in Utah, the white snow on the ground was beautiful, but only seemed to add to the chill in my heart. Life was so much easier when we lived in California. Of course, we had not faced the challenges we met when we moved to Utah, challenges that would have come no matter where we lived.

I was gloomily thinking about the fact that my Kevin would have his first Christmas in Utah hooked up to a dialysis machine. Even though he was free during the day, all I could picture was his little frame lying in his crib, with this long plastic tube coming out from his tummy and into the metal machine we named Mr. Robot. How I wished that things could be different. How I prayed for a miracle of healing for my son.

You might say I became obsessed in my thoughts about it. I mean I couldn't even sit in church next to a family whose children were the same age as Kevin because their children were healthy, and mine was not. I ached for the healing hands of Jesus to touch my son's little body and to make him whole again.

Suddenly, I heard the words, "Carrie, seek my face more than my hands." Turning around to see if Jeff had entered the room, I shook my head and brushed the thought away. But it came again. "Seek my face more than my hands." Realizing the words had come from within my spirit, I knew the Lord had spoken to me to guide and bring me back to the path He had prepared for me.

I felt something in my heart soften. It was the most wonderful feeling; all the grief and the disappointment seemed to just melt away like butter. I didn't feel the jagged edge of sharp pain anymore. I think I must have surrendered something dear and precious to me, as I saw myself lay Kevin on the altar and say, "Okay, Lord. I shall. I will trust You. I will learn to seek who you are, more than what you can do for my son." I had had an epiphany. I remember walking, or rather floating, into the kitchen and Jeff saw my face. He asked me what happened. I couldn't quite describe the whole event, but something inside me had changed. I felt quieted by this experience, finally at rest.

Through the course of the year, as we waited for the next transplant, I waited in peace. I was learning about who He was by seeking His face, and left the worry of it all in His Hands- His scarred, beautiful, healing hands of love.

"I have learned the secret of being content in any and every situation; I can do everything through him who gives me strength." (Philippians 4:11, 13)

Several months after the
failed transplant,
God's sweet "NO" to my
Request was better than
"YES!"

13

Timing is Everything

*T*here are different types of waiting room experiences in life. Some are literal waiting rooms – at a doctor's office, business office, or hospital. Other waiting rooms are more of a metaphor we use to describe our situation in life. We wait for circumstance, timing, people, and the right combination of events to fall into place to fulfill a dream in this type of waiting room. One particular waiting room experience of this kind comes to mind as I reflect back on the day our friend Alex, from Florida, called.

Alex was calling to tell us that a very close friend of his was in the hospital in critical condition. She was not expected to live, and her husband had discussed with Alex the possibility of donating her organs in the event of her death. Alex knew that Kevin's first transplant had not been successful and that he had been waiting several months for a new kidney to become available. As delicately as he could, Alex shared Kevin's story with his friend whose wife's condition was on the critical list. Alex said he seemed deep in thought and appeared to not have heard a single word.

Hours later, as they huddled together waiting for the next update on his wife's condition, they learned she had taken a turn for the worse and her organs were beginning to shut down. The doctors needed to know the family's wishes; timing was critical. Quietly, with determination, the husband told the doctor to give her kidney to a young boy in Salt Lake City, our son Kevin. It was at this moment that I received the phone call from Alex, one I will always remember, and a day I will never forget.

As Alex presented this incredibly generous offer, I wondered if this was even feasible. I told Alex I needed to make some phone calls, making inquiry first with the National Kidney Donor Organization to learn if this would be acceptable protocol. Although Kevin was not at the top of the national list to receive a kidney, exceptions could be made in extenuating circumstances, like these. I called Alex back and let him know that yes, we could do this and gave him the information to make the necessary arrangements for cross checking blood samples. A series of phone calls, faxes, and medical data were exchanged between Utah and Florida at an amazing rate of speed. The transplant coordinator called to advise me that Kevin should not be given any food or drink until further notice, in case he would be taken to surgery that day. How do you keep a two year-old from having lunch or a drink from his favorite tippy tumbler? I worried about this then decided I needed extra help, so I did the only left to do...pray!

For the next several hours, I was amazed that Kevin was content to simply lie on the couch with his white blankie and watch Sesame Street...without eating or drinking! I, on the other hand, could not sit still, and found myself on an emotional roller coaster that wanted to leave the tracks. Adrenaline, fear, hope, excitement, and dread ricocheted around in my thoughts like bullets flying and bouncing off a steel wall. I was in utter amazement as I contemplated that in one moment, after months of waiting, one phone call could so dramatically change our lives. Kevin would finally have the kidney he needed to live a better life. It was the day we all longed for, hoped for, and prayed for. Now that it was here, I wasn't sure I wanted it to happen.

Luckily, Kevin had his blood drawn just the day before so the hospital had all the samples they needed to run the necessary tests over the course of the next five hours. The phone must have rung every thirty minutes, updating me on the latest developments as well as the nurse calling to check and see how Kevin's blood pressure was doing that day. We had formed a habit of making sure the Jeep had a full tank of gas at all times so we would always be ready to make the drive to the hospital when THE phone call came. It gave me a little comfort knowing we were ready to roll if need be. Jeff was flying a trip, so I couldn't even reach him for a few hours to let him know about these events.

To keep busy and to try and calm myself, I decided to turn my attention to the food pantry. A rather large, oversized closet which I knew would create a project that would keep my mind busy for a while. Taking everything down off the shelves, I made groupings of items that went together, like a well organized fashion wardrobe. Using my fancy calligraphy pen, I wrote labels for the items and taped them on the shelves. Decorative baskets contained small packets of sauces, spices, and the like. It was beginning to look like a carefully planned store window, as I separated food categories into an attractive display. Oriental food, Italian, soups, rice and pasta were center stage.

Every so often Kevin would pad his little way into the kitchen, look into the pantry and exclaim, "That looks really nice, Mommy. I like it!" Sucking his thumb with his blankie trailing behind him across the kitchen floor, he'd wander back into the living room and crawl up on the sofa. Once, he asked me if he could have a drink, but didn't fuss when I said, "Not yet, honey. Pretty soon Mommy will get you one." The hours wore on and the pantry was transformed into a work of kitchen art.

As I stood back admiring my hard work, the phone rang. Something about it ringing at this time, when I was all done with my self-invented project, made my hair stand on end. I seemed to sense this was the call that would tell it all. As my heart pounded in my ears, I reached for the phone. "Mrs. George? We're so sorry, but the match is not compatible with your son." The voice droned on with far too many details explaining their findings, but I didn't care. I thanked her politely and slowly hung up.

A surge of relief washed over me like a cool ocean wave on a hot summer day. We were not going to do surgery today! Kevin would not be getting a new kidney. Jeff would not have to fly home on emergency status. It was over, for now. I was never so happy to hear the word... "no."

I fixed Kevin all his favorite foods, filled his favorite tippy cup, and rushed in to join him and watch our favorite video, Winnie the Pooh.

I realized probably for the first time since Kevin's failed transplant that our family needed more time to heal, that we weren't ready to go through another major ordeal quite yet. I am so glad God knows us so well. I have heard it said, "Be careful what you pray for, you just might get it!" I have learned now to say thank you when His answer seems to be no. I know that it sometimes means...not now.

Jesus has a toll-free number....

P R A Y E R

7 7 2 9 3 7

14

The 25 Cent Prayer Chain

When six out of six surgeries failed, we found ourselves asking, "Is there something about prayer that we don't know? Did praying really help, anyway?" It did not appear to change the outcome; it seemed we were destined for doom. We had looked to God for our answers and for every decision we faced. We prayed for the right doctors and for the right hospitals. We had flown Kevin across the country, trying to find the right specialist who would give us the right results. All we wanted was to see our son get well, and yet the desired outcome eluded us. Tears and fears and sleepless nights wore on, while days and weeks of questions formed. Our riverbank of prayers had run dry.

Kevin's fourth surgery was to be a kidney transplant, a gift of health from his father. In spite of the fact he was just two years old at the time, Jeff and Kevin were thought to be a good match. We were quoted a ninety-five percent success rate for living related donors. Unfortunately, he fell into that small, five percent category and our dream of seeing our son healthy was put on hold when he acutely rejected Jeff's kidney that same week that it had been transplanted. Instead, we brought our son home one month later, to a new way of living. A kidney dialysis machine became the means of life until a new kidney became available.

Finally, after eighteen months of waiting and performing dialysis at home, a cadaveric kidney was found for Kevin. A family who had lost their daughter in a car accident generously looked beyond their own tragedy and offered the gift of her organs to several patients like Kevin. I marveled at the selfless gift of their daughter's organ, one which would help my son live. I could not help but wonder if this would be another failure like the one before. On the other hand, maybe we were about to realize our deepest longing come true. Would Kevin now be able to live normally like all the other boys his age, without being hooked up to a machine? "Oh Lord," I prayed, "Show us what to do!" I have heard when you don't know what to do, don't do anything. But we did not have that luxury; time was of the essence. So we took a huge leap of faith, committing it to the Lord, trusting Him with the outcome. It was not easy to do, especially when there had been failures in the past.

This second transplant went well, and I noticed a new feeling rising up inside me, as if we had just been given a new beginning. But I was afraid to get my hopes up, so I kept forcing this bubble of joy back down. Every time my heart would surge with hope, the doctor would come in reporting that there was concern about the kidney function. These announcements would bring me back down emotionally to a place I was more familiar: disappointment and fear. At times the concern would be for the decrease of urine output, at others, for the blood pressure elevation, and at others, for the blood flow to the kidney. Rising and falling with each report, my faith went on a roller coaster ride. Sometimes I wondered if the doctor suspected that I had people praying; maybe he noticed the positive results which followed his negative concerns. Every detail was covered with prayer. I recalled the verse: "I watch over my Word to perform it." (Jeremiah 1:12.) With renewed faith, I would search my purse, retrieve a quarter, and head towards the pay phone to call the prayer chain at our church.

Although it seemed as if our prayers simply bounced off the walls since the time of his first transplant, they provided incredible peace with this one. Somehow, I sensed that no matter what happened, God was in control, and I was learning to simply let go of my fears and trust Him. With quarter in hand heading towards the pay phone, Jeff would ask, "Where are you going?" "To call the Prayer Chain from church," I would reply. Jeff queried: "What for? Why bother these people with all the details? It doesn't make any difference anyway." I had thought to myself as I dialed the number, "He could be right. After all, it did not seem to make much difference before, but I have to try. What is there to lose?" I placed my calls, briefly filling them in on the latest information, then returned to Kevin's bedside to monitor the results. Within the hour, the urine output increased…a good sign. Another time, the blood pressure came down to normal range. Then another time, an ultra sound showed that the blood flow to the kidney had improved to an encouraging rate. Amazingly, every detail from every update was answered through prayer. Jeff started to take note of the 25¢ prayers.

The days wore on, and Jeff still had not prayed. Although he never said a word he seemed doubtful and distrusting of the positive results we were seeing first hand. The doctor would come in and report his findings, and if things did not look just right, I would fish into my purse, find another quarter and head towards the phone. Jeff would just roll his eyes and would shake his head, worrying that I bothered them too much.

Ten days after the transplant surgery, we pulled into our usual space in the all too familiar hospital parking structure. As I reached for the door handle and began to open it, Jeff put his hand on my shoulder and asked, "Aren't we going to pray first?" It had been months since Jeff and I had prayed together as a couple; he had given up on the idea of asking for God's help. *Did he just ask if we could pray?* Inside, my heart pounded with adrenaline and hope. Outside, I pretended to be cool, not wanting to embarrass him. I simply smiled and bowed my head, and said, "Sure!" I gently closed the door and felt the warmth of my own tears run down my cheeks. This holy moment we shared was a dream which had finally come true. The riverbed of prayer had not run dry. It had just taken a turn around a new bend.

.

Your life may be the only Bible someone reads!

15

Easter Saves Bunny

*B*unny was an extremely bright young woman who was also a strong athlete. A resident doctor specializing in sports medicine, she was about to become well trained in an area she had not previously considered…by a small, two year old kidney patient named Kevin. Dr. Bunny had heard about Kevin from one of her colleagues, Dr. White, who had assisted in Kevin's kidney transplant. He had been talking to her about the young boy's failed surgery and the complications and trauma he had gone through at such an early age. Dr. White took notice that, despite all the setbacks, Kevin always seemed to come through with a quiet, cheerful attitude. Bunny could tell from the way her colleague talked about him that Kevin had gotten under his skin and into his heart.

One morning, intrigued by their unusual bond, Dr. Bunny decided to drop by Kevin's room and pay him a visit. She arrived at five thirty a.m., an hour before her shift. Entering his room she found him already awake and lying in his crib. "Hi Kevin, I'm Bunny!" As he lay there sucking his thumb, Kevin gave her a winning smile, liking the sound of her name. She found she could talk easily with this young man and the two of them became instant friends.

It wasn't long before visiting Kevin became part of her morning ritual. She would arrive early at the hospital, climb the stairs to the third floor, and plop her backpack down on the foot of his bed. It became a game for them. He would ask her what was in her backpack, and she would let him reach inside and retrieve the book of the day. Laughing, reading, and turning pages together, they passed time quickly...she would let Kevin play with her stethoscope, and Kevin would talk about his good friend Jesus, telling her about the times he saw Him in the hospital room with him. She said that Kevin was teaching her things that medical training had not. More and more, she found herself looking forward to their next visit.

Eventually, Kevin came home and Bunny continued visiting him. Bright and early on February 4, 1990, a year and a half after meeting Kevin, Bunny was paged while skiing in Snowbird. Her friend, Dr. White, was calling from the hospital to let her know that a new kidney had been found for her little friend Kevin and transplant surgery was scheduled for later that morning.

Bunny finished her run, snapped off her skis, and ran to her car. She said she drove so fast down the mountain that she was surprised she didn't lose control of her car on the icy turns. Still dressed in her ski clothes, Bunny hastily scrubbed and entered the Pre-Op area with Kevin's favorite book, Oh the Places You'll Go by Dr. Seuss, under her arm. Kevin had confided in her that surgery wasn't scary, but he really didn't like the part when they put the mask on his face. His courage had touched a special place in her heart. Bunny decided that she needed to be with him at the time they prepared him for surgery so she could read his favorite story to him while he drifted off to sleep.

Bunny came through the O.R. doors beaming with pride. "I got to be with my little buddy while they put the mask on his face and he did great!" It meant a lot to her to be able to do this for him, not to mention what it meant to us knowing he had a friendly face by his side at that moment.

As the months wore on, Bunny would stop by the house to visit her favorite friend with his new kidney. Somehow, the conversation turned to spiritual matters and we found ourselves talking about God. I told her about my relationship with Jesus and how He gave me peace and strength, especially during times of crisis with Kevin's surgeries. After Bunny left, I sensed that our conversation introduced a new conflict in her analytical mind. How would she satisfy her need for scientific evidence when, clearly, this would require her to rely on something as intangible as faith?

A few days later, Bunny called wanting to know if she could come to church with us the following day, Easter Sunday? As the worship music played, I saw, from the corner of my eye, tears rolling down her face. She was leaning forward in her seat, listening intently to the Easter message. As the pastor closed, he invited anyone who would like to pray with him to come forward, explaining the message of free salvation and the true meaning of Easter.

Bunny turned to me and whispered, "Will you go up with me?" Tears quickly filled my own eyes as I realized how deeply the Lord had been moving in her heart all these months. She was now ready to give her life to the Lord, and as the pastor prayed with her, a peaceful glow washed over her face.

Bunny was baptized in our spa with friends and leaders from our church. When asked to give her testimony that Sunday, she humbled me with her words: "I've watched the George family for over a year now, and have seen them go through serious trials. But there was something different about them, the way they handled things. And there was no mistaking that Kevin's joy... was just not of this earth. That made me know God was real. I saw that He was real in their lives and now I believe."

"Consider it pure joy, whenever you face trials of many kinds," (James 1:2) There is no greater joy than seeing one give their heart to the Lord and, if he uses the backdrop of grief in our family's lives, we are grateful. From a young boy's crib, the heart of God reached out to a doctor we'll always remember...Bunny!

While sitting on an airplane,
A vision I did see...
One which seemed so pleasant,
A waiting room filled
With angels
And
Me!

16

The Waiting Room Vision

*I*t's a quiet place, serene...but seems noisy due to the large number of guests here. Our Host has been so gracious. His angel servants minister so sweetly as they offer a variety of appetizers to hold us over while we await the "great meal" of our hearts' desire. Won't you try one? Today's delicacy is called "Petafours of Humility." You must let it melt in your mouth, rather than bite into it. That way, you can savor the rich flavor and receive the fullness of its benefits to your soul. It actually causes you to forget that you're in....The Waiting Room.

A simple diagnosis
From a complicated source
Our Heavenly
Physician knows
How to steer our course.

Always pray that your doctor be given the mind of Christ, that the Heavenly Physician would impart divine wisdom to his mind and bring the proper diagnosis and care.

17

Night in the ER

"And the peace that transcends all understanding shall guard your heart and mind in Christ Jesus." (Phillipians 4:7)

Very early one dark morning, a few months after the transplant, Kevin awoke crying. Hurrying to his room I felt breathless as the adrenaline kicked in. "Now what, Lord?"

Kevin felt hot, so I took his temperature. It was 101 degrees. He complained of pain somewhere in his belly, one of the dreaded symptoms of rejection. Having been down this road before, fear gripped my heart as I thought about the possibility of another failed transplant.

Jeff came into Kevin's room and decided we should pray. Listening to Jeff as he pleaded on our son's behalf to the Lord, I felt strengthened and faith took over. Somehow I knew that this would be a long night and that we were in a spiritual battle. Although the symptoms were real and natural, I sensed that this would be a battle in a spiritual realm which could only be won on our knees.

After praying, Jeff called the doctor and was told that if his fever did not come down in an hour, we were to bring Kevin to the Emergency Room for evaluation.

I've never wanted to call anyone at such an ungodly hour, but I felt a strong urgency that we needed help with prayer. I called our friend Ron Scarpa, and he offered to come over. True to his promise, Ron and two elders from our church arrived and we began to seek the Lord for His wisdom.

The fever continued to rise, so we packed a few items for the drive to the hospital. I hurried downstairs to Jason's room and let him know we were taking Kevin to the Emergency Room. "Tell Kevin I'll see him when he gets home" he said sleepily. As we rounded the curves along the base of the Wasatch Mountains, a boldness and confidence came over me so strongly that I didn't recognize myself. It was unusual for me to feel this way in crisis. I know this sounds funny, but I actually heard in my thoughts that this was not rejection, but merely a severe case of constipation. I kept this personal revelation to myself for the time being.

One of the doctors from the kidney team met us in an examining room and it was her opinion that Kevin possibly had appendicitis. She called the O.R. and had them standing by and told us that Kevin would need an emergency appendectomy. Jeff and I both felt unsettled about this abrupt decision, so I searched my purse for some quarters and headed to the pay phone. The wonderful prayer chain people were on their knees for our son once more.

When I re-entered the room, the doctor was not there, so I quickly shared my theory with Jeff that it was not appendicitis, just a bad case of constipation. Jeff asked, "Are you sure?" No, I wasn't sure, but it felt right. There was a strong assurance of it deep in my heart. I didn't have anything to base this on other than this unrelenting thought which came during our prayer time with the elders. It sounded silly even to my own ears; to say it was only constipation when there could have been far more serious things going on. I felt enormous pressure. What if I was wrong? His life was at stake!

Thanks to hospital protocol, I did not have to worry about making the decision. Kevin's transplant surgeon, Dr. Nelson, had to be notified before any surgery could be performed on Kevin. Kevin was still officially under his care, so no one could touch our son without his approval. He arrived at the ER shortly after 4:00 a.m. to assess the situation with Kevin.

Worried that he would agree with the other doctor's diagnosis, there was an awkward silence as we waited for him to speak. Dr.

Nelson calmly said: "Well, I see no need to rush Kevin in to surgery just yet." What a relief! Then, he surprised us by turning his attention to me and inquired: "Mom, what do you think it is?" Embarrassed to say what I thought, I shyly stated that I thought it was a matter of constipation and, although I did not have any medical training, I did not believe his appendix was involved.

"Well, Mom, you may be right. Let's wait an hour and I'll check back on him." With that, he left the room, and now the kidney doctor was angry with me. There had been a tension between the two doctors, and the fact that he conferred with me made it awkward. Turning to me, the doctor fired the question: "Mrs. George, do you realize that your son could die if his appendix burst? His body is immuno-suppressed, the poison could kill him!" I felt the sting of her words and faltered. But a moment later, that quiet peace and assurance returned. I told her that I absolutely wanted no harm to come to my son, and that I respected her opinion as a trained physician. But as Kevin's mom, I just felt that for some reason Kevin would not need surgery this morning. She turned on her heels and left the room in a huff, and I certainly understood her frustration with me. But when God shows you something, there's no way to explain it. It's just settled!

Dr. Nelson came back and checked Kevin several times, and eventually even ordered him a room so we would be more comfortable. It had been a long night. Thankfully, surgery was not required, only a laxative and a little time. Dr. Nelson walked in later that morning and chuckled, "Mom, maybe we ought to make you a doctor, you made the right diagnosis. I guess you were right after all." No, not me but the One who knows us best sure did.

Note: Thirteen years later, we had dinner with Dr. Nelson and his wife. Seeing Kevin doing so well after all these years made for a happy occasion.

Miracles still come to us
in many forms:
Such as physical,
emotional and spiritual.
But the greatest miracle of all,
is a life that has
Been touched and
transformed by the power
Of God's love.

18

Derek's Miracle

Psalm 41:3 "The Lord will sustain him on his sickbed and restore him from his bed of illness."

*I*t was the night of the second transplant, February 4, 1990. Kevin had been in surgery earlier that day and was resting comfortably in the Intensive Care Unit. As he was contentedly sucking his thumb in his sleep, we decided to sneak out and grab some dinner. It had been a long day, and we were tired but excited. The history of failed surgeries and one unsuccessful transplant dominated our thoughts and yet the hope for healing empowered us. The Lord had faithfully seen us through the dark storms, maybe now He would show us the rainbow.

We shared our dinner with our favorite doctor and friend, Dr. Tom. He had assisted in four of Kevin's surgeries. We were like family by now and felt comfortable leaving the hospital to have dinner with him, especially since he brought his cell phone along. He would call the unit every half hour to check on his little patient, and assure us that all was going well. How many families get this kind of a blessing? Rare, I know.

After dinner, I walked through the double doors of the ICU and as I rounded the nurses' station and to head towards Kevin's room, I noticed a woman in one of the glass units. She was sitting in a rocking chair alongside her son's bed and I felt drawn to her for some reason. She was a young mother who clearly looked distraught and alone. I did not want to intrude, after all, this was the Intensive Care Unit and you don't just go into another patient's room uninvited. But I could not resist the urge to go in and check on her.

Tip toeing in, I knelt down beside her chair and whispered: "Is there anything I can do for you? My son is in here, too." I said. She looked at me with her blue tearful eyes and asked: "Well, yes. My family left two days ago to return to Idaho and I don't know anyone here. Do you know a pastor who might come and pray for my son?" She then explained that she had donated her kidney to Derek 10 days ago, and the transplant was going so well that the family members left ahead of her to go prepare for his homecoming. But things suddenly took a turn for the worst, and his body was rejecting the kidney. Having been down this road ourselves, I decided it was best not to share our story, as I knew it would discourage her. She said that they had given her son a large dose of OKT-3 to try to stop the rejection, but it didn't work. He was scheduled to have surgery tomorrow morning to remove the kidney and then be placed on dialysis.

My heart really went out to her. I knew firsthand the anguish she was feeling. Wanting to encourage her, I kept the failure of Kevin's first transplant out of our conversation and agreed that there is much power in prayer. I told her I would ask my pastor to come and pray, and see what the Lord would do.

After placing the call to him, it wasn't long before our pastor and an elder of our church quietly entered Derek's room. It almost felt like a heavenly presence came with them. With hearts ready to pray, and a vial of oil in hand, we began to lay hands on Derek and call upon the Name of Jesus, our Healer. Their compassion and tenderness towards Derek and his mom made me want to cry. We asked in the Name of Jesus, that this boy would be healed, the rejection would be reversed, and the transplant would be accepted by his body. We prayed for his mom and felt the peace that only God can bring in those times. Leaving her room, I returned to my own son's bedside and worried over him, wondering what his outcome would be.

The next morning, I returned to the hospital and just as I was about to go past the nurse's station, Gaye came flying out of the room towards me. Throwing her arms around me, she cried: "It's a miracle, it's a miracle! They said that his kidney is working again and the levels are coming back down. All night long, they drew blood from him every hour to see if what they were seeing was true, and now they have cancelled the surgery for the morning."

We rejoiced together in front of the nurses and shared the bond only mothers understand. Her son was going to be alright. I wondered if I dared hope the same for mine.

Well, the days wore on and we became like family. I had offered to take her wash home with me at night, and in the morning I would return with it, neatly stacked and folded like a Chinese laundry. We brought them food and offered them a place to stay in our home once he was released, so he could grow stronger for the long ride home. It was one of the richest times in our lives, being able to minister to another family, while we ourselves were also in need. This is what the Lord definitely wanted to use in and through our family's life...to comfort others with the comfort that we had received.

Although it would be a tumultuous two years of rejection episodes, anxious rides to the Emergency Room with Kevin, and juggling medicine around, eventually our lives settled down into a routine and the healing did come. Not without struggle, and not without tears, but it came over time...and it was worth every fear. We learned to face the fear of rejection, as well as the fear of losing our son, and we learned to reach for faith in the midst of it all.

I love the saying "I never said it would be easy, I said I would be there." This sums up the truth for me in no better way. He is there with you, too.

The God of the impossible turns things around, He blesses you with grace and transforms your mourning into crowns.

19

Precursor to Hide and Seek

*D*uring a difficult phase of our marriage, I found peace in the Lord's love. As I turned to His Word, His strength comforted me. He seemed to draw me closer to His heart, holding me tenderly through this time of loneliness. I didn't want my need to be comforted by Jeff to exceed my need of finding comfort from my Lord. Oftentimes I would quote scripture aloud to encourage myself. A special scripture during that time was from Psalm 91. I envisioned myself hiding under the shadow of his wings and seeking El Shaddai. Paraphrasing this verse, I personalized this scripture and it became my daily prayer.

"She who dwells in the shelter of the Most High will rest in the shadow of the Almighty. I will say of the Lord, 'He is my refuge and my fortress, my God, in whom I trust.' Because she loves me, says the Lord, 'I will rescue her; I will protect her, for she acknowledges my name. She will call upon me, and I will answer her; I will be with her in trouble and I will deliver her and honor her."

20

Hide and Seek

I watched you demonstrate your powerful love for our son. I had not seen this side of you before where raw, unrestrained emotions would briefly escape the tight reign you held them in. The grief and loss you felt mirrored my own inner turmoil yet we were unable to talk about it.

I longed to be a part of the healing process with you but realized we would have to do this on our own separately for the first time. I did not know how to find a path of healing without you yet understood that we needed to go through this individually. Instead of connecting with me, you reached for our son to comfort your tormented heart. I hurt too. I lay awake at night wondering if this would go on forever and eventually cause us to drift apart. I trembled at the thought that the wonderful marriage we once shared might not survive the darkest storm of our life.

I felt the distance growing between us by the far away look in your eyes. My prayers to God became my anchor of hope, giving me the courage to wait. As you slowly found your way, I found mine too. I believe heaven sent a light and shined it on the right course for us to heal. Otherwise we would have missed the best that was yet to come. I love you, my husband friend.

Black Diamond Run
A Trail to His Plan

21

Glen's Story

"*I* just received a call this morning from a church in Boise, Idaho," Pastor Bill announced from the pulpit one Sunday in January. "They need our help praying for one of their young members named Glen, who was skiing here while on winter break from college." "He's had a terrible accident and is listed in critical condition with a broken neck. His parents flew in last night and don't know anyone here and I'm sure they would welcome your support and prayers."

Glen's condition was grave and there was concern as to whether he would make it through the night. As our pastor related the plight of this family, my husband Jeff was deeply moved. Although fortunate to have no permanent injury, he recalled the fear he felt years ago when the doctor told him he had broken his neck.

An expert skier, Glen wanted to finish a great day of skiing by taking his last run down a newly opened Black Diamond trail. Glen knew he had to conquer this hill before hanging up his skis. As he stood at the top taking in the sight of the daunting down hill course, he could not see the shaded area covering the danger which awaited him. Glen started his descent, and as the wind whipped through his hair, the increasing speed of his skis sent a thrill through his body.

Suddenly, without warning, the soft, graceful sound of his skis turned to a grating, icy, sickening one. Scraping over rugged exposed rocks, Glen lost control and went sailing head over heels, his head crashing into a boulder. Moments later, Glen was discovered by the Ski Patrol lying in a pool of blood. The sight they came upon was gruesome. They worked quickly to stop the bleeding and immediately arranged for him to be life-flighted to the closest hospital.

While Pastor Bill continued sharing, Jeff leaned over and whispered: "Can you go see them at the hospital today and let the family know I'll be up there as soon as I get home from flying this trip?" I agreed to go even though I felt uncomfortable visiting people I'd never met in such grave circumstances.

As I walked into the room, I felt the questioning gaze of Glen's father. Probably, he was wondering who I was, but I interpreted his look to mean that he didn't want an intruder. I felt uneasy with the awkwardness of walking into a stranger's hospital room. Quickly I introduced myself, explaining that I had heard about their son's accident while at church that morning and had come to let them know we were here if they needed anything. I think my visit lasted a total of seven minutes. I could not wait to escape and leave this poor father alone with his son. I gave him our phone number and left.

Having been in the hospital so many times with our own son, I should have realized that any visitor, even unexpected ones, are a breath of fresh air when you've spent hours and days in one small, sterile hospital room. But my own insecurities in an awkward situation got the better of me. Maybe I could bring them some home made cookies on my next visit.

When I got home, they called to thank me for coming and said if we were in the area, to please stop by again. I knew there would be a very good chance of this since Kevin needed to be seen on a regular basis at this hospital. What I didn't know at the time was that our lives were about to blend together sooner than expected.

Two weeks after meeting Glen's family, we received a call from the Transplant Coordinator that a kidney had been found for Kevin. We were on our way to the hospital with our four-year-old son, when I realized that we would be spending more time with Glen and his family, all under the same roof. Somehow that thought comforted me. I would later look back on this time with fond memories. Staying in a hospital with another family has an amazing way of bonding you closely in a very short period of time. After a few short weeks we were home again, but the House family remained at the hospital since Glen would be there for several months.

Wednesday evening services were always a special time where people could come and receive prayer and the teachings were a little more casual. Just as the music started that night, I could hear a commotion in the back of the church. Turning to see what it was, I gasped with surprise. Glen was being rolled down the aisle in a wheelchair by his parents. He had come to thank everyone for their prayers and encouragement over the past several months.

As the service concluded, many well-wishers gathered round Glen's chair and Pastor Bill asked him if he would like to receive prayer. Glen smiled with such grace and humility. For a moment I felt as though Christ's face and eyes were shining through his. "I would ask that the Lord would heal my hands so that I can go to medical school. As it stands right now, I can't move my fingers and would not be able to perform the labs required in order to graduate."

He continued, "God saw fit for me to be in this chair for some reason, and I'm okay with that. But I do want to finish medical school. I know I'm supposed to be a doctor, so I really need the use of my hands."

With that, we all gathered around and laid hands on Glen, our pastor anointed him with oil, and we took turns praying over him. A few minutes into this sacred moment, I opened my eyes to peek and see if anything was happening. Nothing could have prepared me for the wonderful sight my eyes beheld. Gently opening and closing his fingers for the first time since the accident, Glen shed tears as he felt the radiating heat of our Healer touching his hands. I poked his mom, who stood nearby, and though startled by this gesture, when she saw the miracle being displayed before her, she immediately cried out in praise to the Living God.

Fourteen years later, Glen is a husband, father, and yes, he finished medical school. He is now the Medical Director of Rehabilitation at Penrose Hospital in Colorado Springs, Colorado. If ever a story of a broken neck could repair one's faith, Glen's is one that offers hope, courage, and trust in the One who hears and carries us all.

I once heard that one way
of knowing you are in God's will
Is by the peace surrounding
your circumstances.
Everything seems to just click together,
And fits into place nicely.
Well, if that is the case,
Then what I thought was
moving to God's will
Definitely was not looking so good.

22

.

Could this be God's Will?

*D*uring the eighteen months that Kevin was on dialysis, we opened our home to traveling pastors and their families who came to Salt Lake City for conferences. Since we were unable to travel or attend church on Wednesday evenings, we found this to be a wonderful opportunity to meet new people from around the country. One visiting pastor and his wife were from Atlanta, Georgia. We got along so well that we felt like instant family. After staying with us for five days, our hearts were knit together and we promised to visit them one day.

Four weeks later, my husband was faced with a job transfer and his two choices were Texas or Georgia. After much discussion, we decided to try Georgia, sensing this was no coincidence in light of Pastor Rick and Susie Snow's recent visit. Arrangements were made, and while Jeff stayed home with Kevin, I stayed at the Snow's home. They showed me some areas and I fell in love with Peachtree City. The move came together smoothly thanks to the generosity of this family, and they offered to keep our son Jason at their house so he could start school on time while we sold our house in Utah.

The day finally arrived when our furniture was unloaded and over three hundred boxes were moved into our new home. Our family was back under one roof again. Jeff would fly out the next morning from Atlanta to Salt Lake, and finish his last trip there. Kevin woke up not feeling well. Even though he was two years post-transplant, he wasn't out of the woods just yet for potential rejection.

After dropping Jason off for his youth bible study, I felt another Emergency Room trip would be prudent. I realized for the first time I had no idea where the Children's Hospital was. I figured that I would just follow the signs and the Lord would help lead me there. I talked to Him in the car all the way asking Him to guide me by His Spirit, which He did do. I found Egleston Hospital and Kevin and I were soon in the usual five hour holding pattern of the Emergency Room. I worried about Jason; how would he get home? I assumed he would catch a ride with someone. Later, I learned that Jason didn't realize we lived eleven miles away, and he decided he could walk home. This turned out to be a bad decision.

Meanwhile, tests were run and an I.V. was started, Kevin was admitted at one thirty in the morning. Exhausted from the move and now this unplanned trip to the hospital, I was suddenly overcome with fatigue. I gladly accepted the cot offered me so I could lie next to Kevin's crib. Just as I was about to doze off, the phone rang, it was Jeff! "How did you find me?" I was amazed he knew how to track us down from half way across the country. He explained that my brother in law had called letting him know where I was as a result of a phone call I had placed to him earlier that evening. My eyes brimmed with tears as I heard my husband's voice and I told him it had been a long, hard day. In his usual dry manner, he said "Well, that's not the end of your troubles." Irritated by his poor timing for jokes, I told him I didn't appreciate the humor just now, but he insisted that this was no joke. He said my other son was in jail! Stunned, I felt my stomach turn and thought I was about to become ill. The blood literally drained from my face and I felt faint.

"Jason was walking home when some neighbors saw him and, thinking he looked suspicious, called the police. When a cruiser flashed his lights on him, he got scared and ran off the side of the road and tried to hide. He had no identification on him and the police didn't buy his story that he didn't know his address as we had just moved in the day before!" Jeff told me not to worry, that he had already called the jail and learned that he was in his own cell. He would have to spend the night and we could come in the morning to pick him up.

Guilt, helplessness, and desperation hit me like a tidal wave. I cried because I knew I could not leave Kevin tonight. I would just have to trust that the Lord would take care of Jason; I simply was so tired I didn't know what else to do. I fell asleep hard and fast. I counted it a blessing!

While I slept, however, the Snows were on their feet in the middle of the night. After hearing of Jason's situation, the Lord prompted Pastor Rick to go down to the jail. He and Susie bailed our son out of jail at 4:00 a.m. and brought him safely to their home. Although I did not know about this until sometime later the next morning, I am still aware to this day how the Lord keeps a watchful eye even as we sleep. The Lord orchestrates his will and sometimes uses His people during the night. "I will praise the Lord, who counsels me; even at night by heart instructs me." (Psalm 16:7)

The next afternoon Jeff surprised me when he walked through the door of Kevin's hospital room. I thought I was dreaming! It just happened to work out that he had a layover in Atlanta that night. Relieved to have my solid supporter, I collapsed into a heap of tears and he held me in his arms. God is so good, He knows exactly what we need at the moment we need it most. He sent me this gift, to help me get through the next several days.

Five days later we were all home together again and this time, I just knew it would be for good. Having come through a tumultuous time of moving in, surely nothing else could go wrong. I unpacked the remaining boxes, thanking the Lord for our new home and the new place we were living. Thanking Him most of all for showing us His will to be here.

In just a few days my parents would be joining us for our first Thanksgiving here just two weeks after moving in. In spite of the turmoil, we were settled in record time. The beginning of our visit with them was off to a very pleasant start. They really enjoyed the long golf cart rides through the thick cover of Kudzu and Pine Trees growing along the paths.

After coming home from dinner that night, Mom and Dad and Kevin and Jason and I relaxed in the living room while Jeff stood at the kitchen sink about to drink some water. Suddenly, for no apparent reason, his nose began to bleed, and, after excusing himself to the bathroom, he summoned me to bring ice and towels. This went on for a couple of hours and eventually we were off to the Emergency Room.

Georgia was under the worst storm watch of the decade and there were no street lights to guide us as I drove his jeep through the horrendous rain and thunder. As soon as we reached the Emergency Room, Jeff was taken into a room and the doctor packed his nose and sent him home. But Jeff was awake all night, trying to stop the bleeding. Apparently the packing was not helping. Eventually we lay down in the wee hours of the morning and I had drifted off thinking all was well. A few hours later I awoke with a start, Jeff was not in bed! Hurrying to the kitchen, I found my mother sitting at the table and she explained to me that Daddy had taken Jeff to the hospital. I called right away and was told that Jeff would be having surgery in a few minutes. I jumped in the car; Mom stayed at home and got Kevin ready for school while I raced back to the hospital. Nervously I paced back and forth outside the Operating Room doors.

An hour later, the surgeon emerged still wearing his surgical gown and cap. "Mrs. George?" Anxiously I nodded, and was surprised when he smiled. "Your Captain is in good shape, and is resting comfortably." His calm demeanor put me to rest as he continued, "I think if we hadn't stopped that bleeding within another hour, he would not have made it." I had a hard time processing that bit of information, my husband had nearly died? His eyes glanced at my necklace, "I see from the cross you're wearing that you're a Christian?" Again I simply nodded my head; I was too overwhelmed with emotions to speak. "Well, I want you to know that I am too. And every morning before I come into work, I lift up these hands to the Lord and ask Him to bless them, to use them to bring His healing!" Then, he gave me a hug! Imagine, a doctor giving a hug!? I thanked him and I hugged him too. Immediately a strong bond of God's love formed. A friendship and a bond in the Lord that is still on-going today, many years later.

Jeff was kept in a morphine coma state for a week, and I was able to sit quietly by his side, day after day, thanks to my parent's staying at our home to care for our kids. The Lord was so sweet and comforting during that time. On Thanksgiving Day, He led me to one verse which meant so much and gave me such great hope. I felt the Lord speaking to me through Jeremiah 33:6, "Behold, I will bring to it health and healing, and I will heal them; and I will reveal to them an abundance of peace and truth." I knew my Jeff would be okay, and that the Lord would use this experience in some way to help further His purposes in our lives, to bring glory to His Name, and to build a faith unshakeable in us.

A week after Jeff returned home, the phone rang. It was the school office calling to tell me that our son Jason had just been taken by ambulance to the Emergency Room! I thought, "Okay, Lord, now what?" I wrote down the information and drove to the now familiar Emergency Room where Jeff had been. I arrived at the same time as the ambulance, which carried my son. I watched in dismay as they carried him on the gurney, his neck and head in a brace to stabilize him. After a few tests were run, Jason was released, good as new. The injury he sustained from a fellow student who kicked him in the back with steel toe boots had only temporarily paralyzed his legs. Thankfully, he was able to walk to the car with only a slight limp.

In an odd way, I sensed that this was all part of the bigger plan. The Snows staying at our home in Utah was no coincidence. The doctor was divinely ordered by the Lord. How could so many crises happen to one family in one month? And yet, the trials we faced have indeed worked together for good. As a result, we now have a life long friendship with the doctor as well as with Rick and Susie Snow. He was stretching us, for whatever reason, and this process has only brought us closer to Him. Who can explain the exquisite power of the peace of God which keeps us in such comfort through the midst of all the struggles in life? "It is God who arms me with strength and makes my way perfect." (Psalm 18:32)

Nine months gives birth
To a new life
In Christ

23

Rebecca

My older son Jason called me one night to tell me that his fourteen year old friend had been in a terrible accident. While spending the night at her girlfriend's house, the two had decided they'd like to take a ride and see what it was like to be behind the wheel of a car. As they crossed a very busy highway, a big rig truck came barreling down the road and there was no time for him to stop. The truck splintered through the mid section of their automobile, causing severe injury to the girls. Jason's friend Rebecca was in the driver's seat, pinned behind the wheel of the crushed vehicle. After being life-flighted to a nearby hospital in Atlanta, Rebecca was reported in critical condition, and not expected to live through the night. That's when my son called me.

"Mom, can you go and pray for her?" I told him I would be willing to, but I didn't want to intrude on their family, as I didn't know the girl or her mother. I told Jason he could give the mother my phone number and, if she would like me to come and pray, I would be happy to do that. Although Jason was no longer attending church himself, he knew there was power in prayer.

A day passed and I had not heard anything from Rebecca's mother. Late the following afternoon however, while at a neighborhood barbecue, the strongest urge to return home came over me. I told my friends that I had to go home and get something, and that I would be right back. While I drove our little golf cart back to the house, I wondered what I was going home for? Maybe my lipstick, I didn't know for sure, but one thing I knew….the feeling was so strong I couldn't do anything except follow its urgent command. Once inside, I looked around the kitchen and didn't see anything to retrieve, so I looked at our answering machine and noticed the blinking light. I hit the "play" button and heard the following message: "Hi, my name is Susan and your son gave me your phone number. My daughter was in a very serious accident and isn't expected to live and your son said you might come and pray. Could you please come to the Intensive Care Unit? The visiting hours are over at seven p.m." I looked at my watch and it was six-fifteen. I had just enough time to make it if I left immediately. I went back to my neighbors' party and told them of the situation and they all sent me off with hopeful wishes but doubtful looks.

When I stepped off the elevator to the intensive care waiting area, I was stunned by the large number of people waiting in the enormous room. There must have been more than fifty people, all waiting to hear something about their friend or loved one. I realized I had no idea what Susan looked like, or even what her last name was. How would I ever find her? Then it happened. That indescribable peace washed over me and as my eyes scanned the room, a voice inside seemed to whisper, "There she is, that's Mom…Susan." Hesitantly, I walked toward her and asked if her name was Susan. She smiled wearily and said yes, she was Rebecca's mother. Inwardly I sighed with relief, I had heard correctly. She thanked me for coming and then whisked me down the corridor to her daughter's room. As we walked down the white, cold, anaseptic hallway, I told her that while I was in the elevator, my Bible had opened to a verse I thought would encourage her. It said, "Only believe and she shall be healed." (Luke 8:50) I told her that God hears our prayers and that He is the only One who can do the impossible. I did not know what God had in store for Rebecca, only that we could ask Him to heal her and wait and see what He would do.

As we entered her room, I was struck by the enormity of this mother's situation when I saw the condition of her daughter. Her entire body was so swollen it didn't look real. Her white, pasty colored face looked like a porcelain doll. The tubes reaching her arms were the only indicator that a life was being sustained. A tomb-like quality already permeated the atmosphere. I asked the Lord to give me faith to pray for her, and He quieted me with this: "Be still and know that I am God."

Reverently, I walked over to her bed and asked Susan if I could anoint her daughter with oil. She said that would be fine with her, and I gently made the sign of the cross on Rebecca's cold forehead and lightly touched her shoulder. "Father, thank you for this life, and for whatever you have in store. I ask in the precious name of Jesus that you would touch this young girl and heal her according to your great mercy and tenderness, and allow her to live and to serve you for the rest of her life. Lord, the doctors say that she isn't going to make it, "but all things are possible with God." (Matthew 19:26) Lord, I believe you are able. Let it be done according to your will. Amen." As I opened my eyes, I smiled at the new warmth which transformed the room. There was a strong sense that two angels were with us and, when I mentioned this to Susan, she said that a pastor and two of the youths from church had come and prayed earlier and they also said they could feel the presence of two angels. I told Susan I would continue to pray and would come as often as she wanted me to.

Susan and I saw a lot of each other over the next several months. She would often call and fill me in on the latest development and, although Rebecca was still in a coma nine months later, she was still alive despite all the odds against her. So many months had passed; we all wondered if this sleeping girl would ever wake up and see the miracle we dearly longed for.

One year later, I was sitting at a restaurant with my mother in Peachtree City when a girl walked in with her mother. I glanced casually in their direction. Something about the mother looked familiar. Not wanting to stare, I looked back down at my menu and heard a soft voice: "Excuse me, my name is Rebecca. My mother Susan just told me that you were sitting over here and that you were the lady who kept coming and praying over me. I just wanted to thank you."

My mouth dropped open, I felt the hot sting of tears, and I

quickly stood up to hug her. I hugged her and hugged her again. I thanked her for the privilege of meeting her and we both laughed when I remarked how pretty she was. Now that I could see her beautiful dark eyes, which had been closed the whole time I'd known her, and there was a glow of pink on her cheeks, she looked like a new creation; a beautiful young woman. She said she recognized my voice. She had heard me every time I came in to pray and it always gave her peace. She had not known much about God before the accident, but as she lay in a coma for nine months, the Lord was revealing himself to her through her dreams. All the prayers people spoke over her helped her feel His love. She was grateful for His faithfulness, and I was blessed to be a part of His plan.

I'll never forget the night I arrived in that huge waiting room, the room which held a destiny for many unknowns, and the future of a girl named Rebecca which He held in the palm of His hands. I'll always remember that with God, all things are possible.

Isn't it wonderful
To have a Risen Savior
Who is not constrained
By denominational walls?

24

Breaking the Rules
Pastor Rick

Our friend George was in surgery for a brain tumor. His wife Leisa, Pastor Rick, Jeff and I sat in a tiny, airless room that morning. Several hours later another family squeezed into this space, and we all slid over to make room on the couch for them. Visibly upset, the nephew explained that his aunt had suffered a brain aneurysm and was not expected to live.

Their conversation resonated with grave concern; their tears flowed unchecked as they recounted their favorite memories of her. Sensing their need for comfort, Pastor Rick offered to pray with them. At first the sister hesitated, asking, "We're Jewish, do you suppose that matters?" Rick smiled warmly and assured her that God listens to all who pray to him. We all chuckled when the woman said that Rick could be a rabbi for a day. Bowing our heads, we joined our hearts and agreed with his prayer. I took note of the peaceful quality in their "amen" as though something heavy had been lifted from their hearts. As the hours ticked by, we learned a great deal about them and we bonded as we shared this time of waiting together.

The following day, we all huddled together in the same airless space, a room so tiny that we could barely walk past another without squeezing our legs together to let them by. Eventually they asked why we all were there, so Leisa explained that her husband needed surgery for a brain tumor, but she was not worried because the Lord had brought this to George's attention. They sat there fascinated as she continued telling George's story. "One morning while George was drinking coffee and reading his Bible, a thought came to him, that he should have an MRI of his brain. He immediately dismissed this crazy thought but it came back to him twice more."

"George called his doctor that morning and thanks to a cancellation, he was able to schedule one immediately." The following day his doctor called him at home absolutely dumbfounded. "George, you have a brain tumor. How did you know? I mean, you don't have any symptoms, what made you want to have this scan done on your brain?" He explained how this thought kept coming to him and he just felt that he needed to act on it since it would not go away.

A few minutes later the nurse from ICU announced to the family that they could go in and visit for five minutes, allowing one person at a time only. No one but the immediate family would be admitted.

The patient's sister was the first one to her feet, relieved to finally be able to see her. But when she returned to the waiting room, she was trembling. She reported that her sister was in a deep coma and her face showed no signs of life. Pastor Rick suggested that in light of George's story, we could also ask God for His blessing on her too. He asked if she would permit him to go in and anoint her sister with oil and pray over her. Her eyes met his and the hope reflected in them stirred my heart as I recalled a similar situation with our own son at a time of desperate need.

"But will they let you in? You're not immediate family!" "Oh don't worry about me, I'll find a way." And with that, Pastor Rick briskly left the room full of faith, knowing he was one of God's servants...called to pray for the sick. He dodged the nurse rounding the corner and slipped quietly into the woman's room. She lay there white as a sheet, lips already gray, hair limply touching the edge of the pillow case. He anointed her head with oil and prayed that God would touch her and heal her and bring her out of this coma. About that time, he was discovered by the same nurse who barked,

"Immediate family only!" Irritated, she escorted him out of that room ordering that he not come back there again.

Upon his return to the waiting room, we looked at him expectantly and noticed the rascal-like smile forming at the corners of his mouth. "I don't think that nurse is too fond of me," he admitted. "But I really trust that the Lord used that moment for his greater plan, even if I did break the rules," he smiled.

Later that day, we all marveled when we heard the nurse's report. A miracle did happen! She woke up from the coma they said she'd never awaken from, and she whispered that she was going to be okay. It was a slow recovery before returning home, but that day did finally arrive and her family rallied around her, fussing over her as she came through her front door.

Kind of funny when I look back on it, Pastor Rick wasn't the only one who seemed to break the rules that day. Wasn't it God who used the prayer of a Christian pastor to restore the health of a Jewish woman?

25

The Waiting Process

The waiting room is where you sit before being summoned to the inner office. While sitting in the outer office, you prepare your thoughts…sharpening and fine-tuning the question which brought you to this meeting place. An urgency to discuss the matter builds with great tension as every thought crystallizes into clear concise thinking. As you intensely strain towards the answer, the door suddenly opens, your name is called, and you quickly rise to your feet.

Once inside, you sit and wait in the final phase of this process. An answer is about to be given…the key of truth will turn and unlock pent up fears and worries. This is a key meeting – a diagnosis may be given, or a prognosis pronounced. Perhaps even a greater understanding will shed light on the need. You wait anxiously to see the one with whom you've scheduled this time.

Whether your waiting room is actual or metaphorical, it is a place that causes discomfort and stretches one to grow. How we respond changes over time as the process slowly rounds off the sharp edges of impatience and a demand to have our own way. Isn't it good to know that He is always there waiting with you?

A missing son
Turns up
Under the
Steady gaze of
The One who sees all...

26

Looking for Jason

"Unless the Lord had given me help, I would soon have dwelt in the silence of death. When I said, 'My foot is slipping,' your love, O Lord, supported me. When anxiety was great within me, your consolation brought joy to my soul." (Psalm 94:17-19)

Jason's friends from church came to us one night because they were worried about him. They confided that he had been taking some pretty hard drugs again, and was hanging out with a guy who was talking about having an out of body experience. As Jeff and I sat listening to them, their voices suddenly grew quiet. Taking a deep breath as though gathering his courage, his friend continued: "Jason also mentioned something about suicide…"

Reeling from the sudden impact of his words, my mouth felt dry as cotton, I was speechless. Not knowing what to do or say, the awkward silence was finally broken by Jeff's soft voice. He began asking questions which unleashed pent up fears and concerns too great for such young hearts to carry. Truth spilled out and fear rose up. Their information was more than we had bargained for, much more than we wanted to know. We thanked the kids for their courage in coming to us and for their love for our son. Then we did what seemed the natural thing to do at the time, we asked them to pray with us. Never had my ears ever heard such tender yet forceful prayers. In spite of their news, we were blessed by their hearts. We knew this was beyond us, a problem only the Lord could handle.

After a sleepless night, I was startled by the front door bell and rushed to see who was there. Hoping to see Jason's face, I was greeted by the kind eyes of our youth pastor, Alan and my disappointment immediately turned to comfort. Sensing that neither Jeff nor I had slept, he offered to drive around and see if he could possibly find Jason. He knew where Jason hung out, but he also was aware of certain underpasses and bridges where teenagers were found. Immediately I knew he meant where their bodies were found, a picture I could not bear.

Not wanting to park my thoughts where gloomy images can overshadow faith, I allowed my mind to travel to a more pleasant time. It took me back to one of my favorite scenes when Jason was just a toddler. Jason's curly bright blonde hair and wiry little body running up and down the beach in Mission Bay, San Diego playing "catch me" warmed my heart. I would pretend to chase hard after him, leaving enough space between us to allow him to get just beyond reach. Suddenly I'd be right at his heels and snatch him up, giving him a brief hug before he'd wriggle free and start off running again. We played this game tirelessly until it was time to go in for lunch.

Focusing back on Alan's intent gaze, the reality of our missing son cut through my daydreaming like a sharp knife. Jeff and I agreed to ride along with Alan as it was better than waiting around doing nothing. Our search began and each time we pulled off the side of the road, I held my breath. Getting out of the car and walking over to the bridge, we would look below for signs of him. Seeing nothing but overgrown weeds and broken bottles, a collective sigh of relief escaped our lips and we continued on to the next location.

Hours later, we returned home. For the time being our search had settled the urgency to do something. Now there was nothing left to do but wait. Alan left and I retreated to my favorite room with my bible. Knowing this to be my only true source of comfort, I looked through the Psalms to see if anything might speak to our situation. As I read the following, I knew my Lord understood my need and was aware of our plight: "Turn to me and have mercy on me; grant your strength to your servant and save the son of your maidservant."

(Psalm 86:16) There was no denying that El Roi, the God who sees, saw our circumstances and indeed had his eye on our son.

Later that evening, Jason's friends called from the Emergency Room to say they had found him at the home of a local drug dealer. Elated by the news, I told his friends we would meet them at the hospital. They discouraged us from coming as Jason was adamant that he did not want his parents to see him this way. They promised they would stay with him and keep an eye on him when he was released. I desperately wanted to hold my son and feel him close to me, to reassure myself that he would be all right. Instead, I had to release him back to the arms of the Heavenly Father. Only He can hold our children when they are away from home.

I will never have the answers as to why some children go astray and find pleasure in a lifestyle so contrary to what they have been taught. But I do know that there is One who says He will never leave us or forsake us, and His Word promises, "Train up a child in the way he should go, and when he is old, he will not depart from it." (Proverbs 22:6) Only the Lord knows how old they will be when they return to the faith they were brought up in, but isn't it good to know that we have a God who sees? He knows all things, and holds all things in His loving hands. We can trust that He cares about our children even more than we do.

Note: Our prodigal son has returned, and we love sharing family time with he and his new wife, Marzia.

Jesus, the Name
above all names
His Name is greater than
Any disease
Any drug
Any affliction

27

If I be Lifted Up

"If I be lifted up, I shall draw all men to myself." Over and over, this verse repeated itself in my mind as the tires rolled along down the highway. The silent drive to the Rehab Center seemed endless, although it was just miles away. We were scheduled to meet with a team of medical professionals to discuss our son's condition and his future.

Jason had been using drugs off and on for a number of years, but now he was into very heavy drugs, like methamphetamine for one. The police had been called when he was discovered swimming naked in a resident's pool while intoxicated. We received a call from the ambulance as it was transporting him to a nearby hospital. We met Jason at the Emergency Room as he was carried in on a stretcher by the paramedics. I'll never forget the dark, glazed look in his eyes, starkly contrasted by the white, crisp canvass he laid on.

As we sat with our son in the small cubical of the E.R., I wondered about many things. Where did I go wrong? The old guilt feelings quickly resurfaced as this drama unfolded before my eyes. When Jason was still an infant, his father had decided he wasn't ready for the commitment of our marriage or raising our son together, a decision he later deeply regretted. Jason and I started our new life by living in my parent's travel trailer parked in San Diego. We were a team now, and the bond between mother and son was thicker than a three stranded cord of gold.

Maybe he felt rejected as he grew older, but he never talked about those feelings with anyone. Maybe that's why he reverted to drugs; to try to bury his pain. Or, maybe it was the fact that I had re-married by the time he was six years old, and learning to share me with someone else was just another blow to his bruised heart. In any case, as he lay there I couldn't help but feel responsible for his drug abuse. He hallucinated several times, talked gibberish, occasionally smiled at some inside joke going on inside his mind. This lasted for the next six hours.

By now, my husband Jeff needed to leave in order to take our son Kevin to the children's hospital for a follow-up appointment. He asked Jason if he could pray for him and Jason seemed to understand and nodded his head yes.

That's when it happened. An indescribable and incredible peace settled over the room, like a warm blanket had been placed over our shoulders. The presence of peace was so real I had to open my eyes to see if perhaps a heavenly being had appeared. For the moment, Jason started to come out of his drugged state and his eyes began to brighten. He looked up at his dad, smiled, and said thank-you. After Jeff left the room, Jason said he was hungry, so I ordered him a sandwich, which he quickly and gratefully devoured.

The Sheriff came in a little while later to escort my son to the state rehab center where he would remain for the next several days. Once he arrived, he would be evaluated and treated accordingly. Apparently, while Jason was in the rehab he experienced several flashbacks, and disturbing images tormented him which he still will not talk about to this day.

The anguish a mother's heart can experience is beyond description. I remember thinking: "if a person could die from a broken heart, this is my time to go!" But I did not die; I continued to live with this weight of sorrow that I was only able to bear because of the peace which came whenever we prayed. Now we were on our way to discuss his prognosis with the psychiatrist, psychologist, drug counselor, social worker, and M.D.

As we walked into that room, the air instantly felt negative, stuffy, and oddly cold, all at the same time. The doctors sat on one side of the round table facing the empty chairs we would occupy.

"Have you prepared yourselves for your son's death?" This was their first opening remark. "It is our opinion that his behavior and unwillingness to admit to his drug abuse will eventually kill him. Have you prepared yourselves for this eventuality?" "Having observed him this week, we feel that his condition is as good as it's going to get." Jason was then pronounced psychotic, detached from reality, unable to carry a conversation due to his short term memory loss as a result of the drugs.

Adrenaline and fear pulsed through my veins and I felt close to blacking out as my heart pounded wildly. Just as I thought I'd surely succumb to the darkness, those words drifted powerfully and swiftly back across my mind. "If I be lifted up, I shall draw all men to myself." That exquisite peace followed the familiar phrase, and although I didn't fully understand it at the time, I knew it was true.

My response startled everyone, especially me. "Well, I believe in miracles and in the power of prayer. We'll see what God has in mind for my son." The legs of the plastic chairs scraped as they were politely pushed back. One doctor cleared his throat and excused himself and others followed. Clearly, I was as much as in denial as my son, or so they thought. Only the drug counselor remained behind. "Keep praying," he whispered to me. The meeting had ended.

It would be several weeks before we'd begin to see our miracle, the healing process of the drugs clearing Jason's system and flushing out of his brain. But the peace that was given to us while we waited was available immediately.

Today, my son is twenty-nine years old, drug free, clear minded, with only a slight deficit of short term memory loss on occasion; a gentle reminder of where he'd been, what he'd come through, and what he'd been saved from. He is a trophy of God's grace, a living example of God's faithfulness. In any circumstance, if we'll lift up His Name in our thoughts and our hearts, He truly does draw us to Himself, in a very special way.

*Waiting
Produces
Its best fruit
When we leave
The results
With God*

28

Heart of a Child

As I sat waiting in the lobby of the drug rehab center to visit with my son Jason, memories of his childhood flashed through my mind. The affection of one particular moment warmed me as thought it just happened. Jason was about sixteen months old at the time and he was racing up and down the short hallway of our travel trailer that we lived in. I had been sitting on the couch playing my guitar, softly singing a song about my broken marriage. Moved by my own sad lyrics, a tear slid down my cheek. Once the first tear escaped, it seemed to make it easier for more to come. It wasn't long before my face was wet and I had to stop playing.

Curious, Jason toddled over to me and with his little hand he touched his finger to my tears. "Mommy cry?" he asked. Nodding my head and scooping him into my arms, I rocked his little frame and held him tightly. His intuitiveness of such a young heart caught me off guard. Although too young to understand, somehow he knew that we were together under special circumstances. Together we would heal all these broken places where divorce had shattered our lives. His innocence was a gift I would fiercely protect over the years but I had no idea that his own feelings of rejection would eventually lead him to drugs.

By the time Jason was thirteen, he dealt with another form of rejection. Our family was suddenly faced with health issues that were overwhelming. This forced us to focus all our energy and attention in one direction; unfortunately it was away from Jason and on Kevin. We were taking Kevin to the hospital routinely while Jason came and went to school. Little did I know at the time, but Jason was silently struggling under the load of his backpack of guilt. Tormenting lies targeted his young mind like an archer's sharp arrow cleverly hitting its target. Each piercing thought penetrated his mind and blamed him for being healthy, strong and athletic while his brother was pale, weak, and sick. Oftentimes the healthy sibling takes on guilt and a sense of responsibility for the illness, feeling certain they must have caused it somehow. This knowledge came to us much later as we delved into therapy with our son. Trying to medicate his inner anguish, he began experimenting with drugs. This began a long cycle of temporary relief for Jason, but as quickly as the drug wore off, the pain reappeared and the need to numb his emotions repeated itself.

Lost in my reverie of past remembrances, his sudden appearance startled me. My eyes quickly assessed his behavior and I was discouraged to see he was still high and in another world. But what was that in his hand? Narrowing my eyes to see what he held, I realize he is carrying the Bible Jeff and I had given him a few years ago. His fingers were holding the page where he must have been reading, and this brought a smile to my lips and a surge of hope to my heart.

Our visit was brief, as he could not keep up with one train of thoughts to carry a conversation. I remember feeling so discouraged on the one hand yet so hopeful on the other. I knew that if he would just turn the pages of his bible, eventually he'd find his path. This waiting room that many parents are in is probably one of the more difficult situations we face. This would seem to be the endless waiting room of prayer, hoping that our children would eventually find their own way. Jason's would be a journey that took ten years of tears, prayers and a roller coaster ride of heartbreaks. It was the most difficult waiting room to occupy. I was waiting for my son to find peace within and to discover the gifts God had blessed him with. Today, it gives me much joy to share with you that Jason is married and in sales, enjoying the value of life and health. I'm so glad I did wait. Never stop hoping, the best is yet to come.

Reframing
The
House
Of
Thoughts

29

Hidden Lies

Waiting rooms can allow the mind to wander into dark corners. The practice of replacing those dark thoughts with the light of scripture has been life-changing for me. When we are ready, and only God knows that sacred timing in our hearts, truth floats down from heaven like a feather cascading gracefully from the sky.

For many years I had tortured myself with the belief that I had somehow caused my son Jason to resort to drugs. Guilt accused me of not showing him enough love, or giving him enough attention, or parenting him correctly.

Another dark, secret thought curled its tentacles around my brain. "If only we had used my kidney" What mother doesn't think that it is her job to give life as well as maintain it? We mothers feel responsible for the well being of our children and for their very breath.

Wanting to be free once and for all from these burdens, I asked the Lord on my fortieth birthday to do the deepest work in my heart that He needed to do in order to bring liberation to my soul. I desperately wanted to have truth because I had come to know that the truth sets us free.

It was months after this prayer that an unexpected answer came. The Lord took me through something I call a breakthrough but psychologist refer to as breakdown. One breathes life and restoration while the other does not. I chose life.

I awakened one morning with a weight like lead on my chest. As the day progressed, the weight grew heavier and I began to think there was something seriously wrong. By evening the tears started, coming from a source of pain I could not identify. I wept bitterly and sobbed at times, not understanding what was happening at the time.

In the morning I thought the grieving was over, but by noontime Jeff found me in my closet weeping all alone. This went on for days. I had no energy; I had no clear thoughts. All I had was this fear that I was losing control and falling apart.

I would get through the days somehow, fixing dinner and helping with homework, but in between the ordinary tasks I would suddenly flee to the bathroom with fresh tears erupting again.

A friend stopped by one day to say hi. Taking one look at me she whispered to Jeff, "Carrie needs help. She needs a counselor." When Jeff suggested her idea to me I felt like I had been slapped across the face. I thought, How dare her! What does she know? But a few days later, desperately afraid, I called a Christian counselor and began my journey to freedom.

I started by telling this counselor that I was a strong person and that I had been handling things just fine all these years, but I suddenly felt the daunting weight of something so heavy I couldn't seem to get out from under its power. He asked me to tell him what was currently going on in my family, so I began to matter-of-factly lay it all out. My husband had just been diagnosed with prostate cancer, my son Jason was in rehab, where the doctors said he might never be right again, and my other son Kevin had been through about nine surgeries and was facing two more in the next few months. "I just don't get it. There's nothing unusual going on, but I suddenly can't seem to cope." As soon as I said it, the look in his eyes told me something I had tried to ignore. It was obvious to him that my thoughts needed some adjusting. I no longer had balanced thinking, being able to weigh what was normal and what was not. Trauma became what was normal for me. I had learned to function under its pressure but my body could no longer perform. Thus, the black veil of depression had engulfed me, trying to swallow me whole.

Weeks later with the tender care and professional skill of the kind counselor, I was beginning to embrace truth again. I began to talk about things that had been buried deep in my heart since I was a child. Feelings of insecurity and unworthiness surfaced from the deepest place and a new resolve to face life rose within me. I was determined to be free and fiercely sought after truth to quench the lies I had believed for so long. I poured over scripture as never before, and it cut through the lies like a sharp two edged sword. The cords were being cut; the shackles were loosening, and several months later... I emerged as a new creation. I looked the same, but everything inside was different. I felt tender and raw, like a burn victim whose new skin was healing from its graft. I didn't want anything of the old to touch the new skin grafts which had formed.

It took nine months of truth in, lies out...learning and relearning. It took another two years to learn how to walk in these new revelations of truth. But with the Word of God, the power of the Spirit, and the prayers of dear friends, I broke through! I was free. Divinely, exquisitely, deliciously free. I was healed. And all the lies, the deceptions, the fears, the anguish, have been replaced with a new mind. "I take every thought captive to the obedience of Christ" and replace negative thoughts with: "Whatever is true, whatever is noble, whatever is right, whatever is pure, whatever is lovely, whatever is admirable-if anything is excellent or praiseworthy- let my mind dwell on these things."(Philippians 4:8)

Clear vision
Comes
When we
Are ready
To see
Truth

30

Healing Waters Clearer Vision

My father and I were sitting together in the waiting room of the Good Samaritan Hospital, while my mother was having surgery for cervical cancer. The close bond between the two of us allowed for the comfort of our silence, but it has not always been this way.

While growing up, Daddy was stern and a strict disciplinarian. He and I had an abrasive relationship during my teenage years, typical of most fathers and daughters. But my sister, Deanna, seemed to hold the key to his heart. At least that was my perception for a number of years.

Deanna seemed to have it all. She was extraordinarily beautiful with olive skin, piercing green eyes, and lush dark curly hair. Everyone loved her; she brought laughter and the light of love with her everywhere she would go. From looking at her beautiful face and radiant smile, it was hard to believe that she could not hear their voices. Deanna had lost her hearing at age four.

Daddy loved both his girls, he always said. But deep in my heart I did not believe it. I felt he loved her more. The summer of my fortieth birthday while vacationing in Hilton Head, Daddy and I had been sitting on the beach together and decided to walk down and get our feet wet. A little boy playing on the beach flung a shovel-full of sand over his shoulders and right into my eyes. The sand burned my eyes so badly I could not open them at all. All I could do was just stand there blinking furiously, hoping the tears would wash out the gritty sand and sting. Unable to see, I was afraid to try to walk.

Then suddenly, I felt his warm hand. Gently, Daddy took me by the arm, and lead me to the water's edge. Carefully, he scooped up the fresh water from the cresting waves and began washing my eyes. It was at this point that I recalled a similar circumstance, which happened two thousand years ago. John 9:6-7 says: "When He had said this, He spat on the ground, and made clay of the spittle, and applied the clay to his eyes, and said to him, 'Go, wash in the pool of Siloam.' And so he went away and washed, and came back seeing.'" I was standing at my own pool of Siloam and was very much like the beggar man who had been born blind. I was in need of the Healer to wash the muddy lies from my own eyes so I could see! The tenderness of my dad's touch and the loving gesture of this simple act melted my heart and cleared my clouded vision forever. That day on the beach the truth exploded inside my heart like a firework crackling in the sky. Daddy loves me. He really loves me!

I smiled at my Dad as he looked up from reading his magazine. Our eyes met as if to say, "Mom's going to be all right." And you know what? She was.

God
Still
Speaks

31

This Too Shall Pass

September morning in Baltimore broke cold, dreary, and wet. Jeff and I boarded the hotel shuttle to Johns Hopkins Hospital, both of us lost in our own thoughts. Today, Jeff would have surgery for prostate cancer, and after the pathologist studied the tissue, we would know if it was too late or if the cancer was caught in time. Neither one of us wanted to admit to the dark fears curling like fingers around our minds as we considered the possible outcome.

All too soon, Jeff was wheeled away through the surgery doors, and I was alone. We had flown to Baltimore from Atlanta because of the doctor's world renowned reputation. But that meant my staying in a hotel alone for a week, while Jeff recovered in the hospital. I didn't know a soul, and suddenly my courage left me and my knees felt like they were about to buckle under.

I was walking down the hall towards the waiting room when a nurse's voice interrupted my thoughts; she had been calling my name. I was remembering that day when Jeff told me he had cancer and how afraid I felt. Yet, after talking it over with the Lord, a peace had settled over me as He seemed to whisper into my heart; "This too shall pass." He had walked us through life threatening circumstances before, and He would be here for us again. Those four little words had comforted me for nearly three months now. But today, I didn't feel comforted. I felt overwhelmed. I was in a city far from home, and my strongest supporter was no longer by my side.

"I'm sorry, what did you say?" I looked at the nurse's face. She was wearing a motherly frown like she wanted to scold me for some reason. She told me that my husband had been so worried about me while she was getting him ready for surgery, that she knew she had to speak with me. So I listened to what she had to say and was amazed by her words.

"Mrs. George, when I was growing up, my grandmother taught me a little saying that always helped her when she was going through hard times. I think you need to learn it, to help you get through hard times." The saying was: "This too shall pass."

Warm tears immediately welled up in my eyes as I heard those words spoken aloud for the first time. Through this nurse's voice, I was reminded that He was here with me today. I gave her a hug and hurried to the waiting room, and, though I was anxious, I was no longer afraid.

The first thing I told Jeff after he came out of surgery was that everything was fine, and the doctor felt that he was able to get all the cancer. Then I told him more good news...that the Lord had shown He was with me in a very special way. Jeff listened as I told him about the nurse and the saying that her grandmother had taught her. This was the first time I told Jeff about the comforting message that had kept me going all summer.

A few years later, we moved from Georgia, to California. Kevin was 13 years old and in need of another surgery to help his transplanted kidney work more efficiently. Even though we had already seen him through eleven surgeries, we still felt like novices when it came to saying good bye as they wheel him through those doors marked Operating Room. Jeff and I leaned over and kissed his forehead, then turned to hide our tears as we walked away.

As we headed towards the car to put away Kevin's belongings, Jeff's cell phone suddenly beeped, alerting him that there was a message waiting. Listening to the call, he turned to me and said, "You have got to listen to this." The message had been left by Caryn, the mother of Kevin's best friend, Wes. Her message said: "I know this is going to sound strange to you because we don't know each other very well. I'm not a religious person, but I was in a very deep sleep when I was awakened by a very strong presence of God in my room." He said to me: "Give a message to Carrie…. "This too shall pass."

Sharing
A room
And a Prayer

32

Nick's Story

*M*ost people hate sharing a room with another patient. The close proximity of the beds, separated only by a curtain, makes privacy impossible. And yet there are times when it's clear that the Lord seems to hand-pick the roommate when there is a bigger plan about to unfold. Nick, who had already been in the hospital for a month, was one such roommate. He had received a liver transplant weeks before, but his body rejected it. A second liver transplant was performed immediately, just a week before our son Kevin became his new roommate. After Kevin had his surgery and returned from the recovery room, our focus was solely on him and we did not talk much to this family for the first day or two.

One morning, Nick's mother was visibly upset and although I did not want to pry, I did ask if there was anything we could do for her. She told us that Nick's blood work from the night before showed that he was going into rejection again, and that it looked like he would be losing yet another transplant. As we talked the nurse came in and drew more blood from Nick and the results were even worse.

I overheard the doctor telling Nick that they would be scheduling him for surgery. They couldn't understand why this was happening again, but the liver would need to be removed. I couldn't help but feel the old, sour taste of our own rejection experience rise up in the back of my throat.

Resisting the temptation to share Kevin's story, I decided to try to encourage her faith. I was uncertain as to whether they believed in God or not but thought I'd just go ahead and tell her about the power of prayer. I carefully explained that there had been plenty of surgery disappointments throughout Kevin's life but one constant remained unchangeable. The peace that would come every time I prayed would give me the strength and courage I needed for the next hour. I told her I prayed often, as there were many challenges, but I needed more strength than I had which I could only find through prayer. I also shared a few stories about how prayer even brought us a few miracles.

By the time we finished talking, she looked over at Nick who had been earnestly listening along. "Nick, what do you think? Would you like this lady to pray for you?" Nick nodded his head yes, so I reached into my purse for the oil that travels with me. I explained that the oil is a symbol of the Holy Spirit and represents His power. I made the sign of the Cross on his forehead, the sign of our Savior and Healer, Jesus. As I prayed, the tears slid down Mom's cheek and Nick's eyes turned wet. One last time he would have his blood drawn before surgery. As they waited for the results, the look in their eyes confirmed that the Lord had touched their hearts. They seemed blanketed in His comfort as if Jesus had wrapped His arms of love around them both.

The results came back and there was a lot of commotion. We left the room to give the nurse and the doctor opportunity to speak with Nick and his Mom privately. Upon returning, the look on their faces told the whole story. His blood work had improved dramatically, surgery was postponed, and there was much hope and excitement circulating like a buzz saw around the room.

I again slipped out of the room to spend some quiet time with the Lord and to thank Him for His amazing faithfulness. For some reason this was a plan that our family was to be part of, teaching us once more to rest in Him. We cannot know what the outcome of our prayers will be, but we can only bring the request to Him and let the answer unfold according to His will.

Later that day, Nick asked his mother, "Mom, how come we don't pray like that lady? Can we do that more?" She told me that she felt God had used this whole rejection episode to get through to her that He is there with them, but they had forgotten to turn to Him. She had been put back in touch with the One who holds all things together in His hand.

Thank you, Jesus. Thank you for caring and for showing us that You are always there.

Steps
Ordered
By the Lord

33

A Divine Prayer Meeting

*A*fter Jeff left for his CT Scan, I went for a walk and decided to find the hospital Chapel. Locating the discreetly hidden room, I gently turned the door knob and tip toed inside. Immediately the sounds of a young man's lamenting cry reached my ears. I paused, wondering if I should leave to allow him some privacy. Oddly, I felt drawn to go inside anyway. The young man quieted himself, seemingly aware that someone had entered the small room.

As I knelt down a few rows behind him, I sensed the presence and power of the Holy Spirit. Uncharacteristic boldness washed over me and I heard myself say: "May I join my prayers with yours?" As if he had been waiting for me, he responded by resuming his prayers, allowing me to enter into this sacred moment with him. The passion of his petition ignited a flame in my heart, confirming that I was to be there praying with this young man. The intensity of his grief for his brother and burden for the lost punctured my own soul. Joining our cries, intercession filled the air. Heaven came down and helped us as we prayed for broken lives to be mended by the loving hands of Jesus. Every need that we prayed for felt familiar, as though what had already existed deep inside my own heart was now given life

The rushing sound of a waterfall of prayer suddenly trickled down to a gentle bubbling stream. Quiet peace settled over the room and we sat in the sweetness of that moment. I was reminded as I sat there of the great power which flows when there is unity in prayer. It was time to leave. We had prayed through all that the Father had placed on our hearts while on our knees.

We hugged as if we were long lost friends, as only brothers and sisters in Christ can do. He introduced himself as Anthony, smiling with a radiant glow. He said that while he was in the chapel the door opened several times, but no one ever came inside. At one point he wanted to leave, but the Lord told him to stay. He was sending someone in to pray with him. He said that when I walked in, he immediately sensed that I was the one who had been sent. It blessed him to see how faithful God was. I admitted my reluctance to enter at first but felt such a strong invitation to join him, I had to obey even though it felt awkward.

I told him that I would see him one day in heaven and that we would know one another by our spirits and he wholeheartedly agreed. Then he took my arm and spoke words which pierced my heart. He said: "The battle will be difficult, but we will overcome!" Nodding my head in agreement, I added: "Jesus never said it would be easy, but that He would be there-"The I Am." Anthony said to keep my eyes on Jesus, and then he turned and left.

Are there angels among us? Yes. And, there certainly are a multitude of saints acting as angels, praying through the trials, difficulties, and storms of life. There are saints among us praying for God's will to be done and for the lost to return to the loving arms of Abba, Father. And sometimes, a divine moment in God's glorious plan brings us face to face, to kneel before Him together, united in spirit and in truth.

Celebrate
Life
In any
And all
Circumstances...

Yes, even in cancer

34

Radiant Anniversary

O n our Twentieth Anniversary, Jeff and I started our celebra-
tion in a most unusual place- the Radiation Oncology
Waiting Room. Surrounded by other cancer patients, we quietly
discussed our plans for the day. Jeff's name was called and during
those 6 minutes of treatment, my mind wandered back to a time
when our marriage was under severe stress.

I remembered where we were standing outside Kevin's room at
the University of Utah hospital when the Social Worker approached
us in her usual no-nonsense manner and said: "I know you and Jeff
have a strong support system here with your church, but I think it
would be a good idea for you to seek some counseling to help walk
you through this transition. Families like yours, who suddenly are
faced with living with a chronically ill child, have a very high
divorce rate. This can place an incredible strain on your marriage
and on your family." I thought she had a lot of nerve to suggest such
a thing to us, and quickly dismissed her counsel. Many months
later, I wished I had not.

Jeff and I had an ideal marriage. All of our friends called us Ken
and Barbie. They said we looked so right together and they could
see how much love there was between us. That's why I never gave it
a second thought that we would experience a marital strain, no
matter what challenges we faced as a family. But what I could not
see at the time was a shadow of darkness that would come and cast

a gloomy depression over my husband's mind. Looking back, it is not surprising that Jeff experienced such a low point. His kidney, which he hoped to save our son, had been rejected and nearly cost Kevin his life. We were donning surgical mask and gloves, hooking our son up to a machine next to his bed instead of just tucking him under the covers to say good night. His best friend had been diagnosed with a brain tumor and died a few months later. A very close uncle died of cancer a few weeks after that, and life seemed very bleak at the time.

In spite of the turmoil, we would continue our ritual of going out to dinner for our date night. But the usual chatter and loving looks were replaced with long silences and empty stares. I did not know this side of Jeff, and I did not enjoy meeting it. Where was my rock and strength? Where was the guy that always made me laugh?

Eventually the depression left, but not without leaving a scar. Not a visible one, but one that etched its ugly mark across the relationship we once cherished, and was now badly bruised. I struggled with the increasing number of things going wrong; a sick child, a wayward son, a depressed husband, and a strain of unspoken misery hung like a thick cloud over our home.

Bringing my broken heart and battered relationship to the foot of the Cross was the only thing I knew to do. Scripture verses, time in prayer, and truthful conversations with my husband rebuilt the bridge of communication and, in time, strengthened the foundation. We found our footing and before long we were walking together as a unified fortress, a strength which can only come after a battle is won.

All these thoughts swirled around in my mind in less than five minutes. Jeff was now walking towards me and as he approached me those deep butterflies I felt back when we dated fluttered to the surface again. "Ready to go?" He asked. We drove to Santa Monica, spent the day walking in and out of stores, having a leisurely lunch at an outdoor café, and then checked into a new and beautiful ocean front resort. Our friends had ordered a stunning arrangement of flowers and chocolate dipped strawberries, adding a special touch of elegance to enhance our day.

Although our lives have been far from easy, we have learned to rest in God. Our future is uncertain, but trusting God and resting in Him allows us the freedom to take one day at a time and to continue to celebrate each day that we have been given. Trusting in a God whose mercy is new every morning gives you the strength to face the mornings, even when radiation awaits you. On this anniversary we realized that the threat of cancer had not extinguished the bright flame burning in our marriage. That is because God's pure light was always kept at the center of our love.

Praying for others
Waters our soul
Like streams of water
In a dry desert

35

Sent To Pray

Waiting Rooms are tolerated by most of us because we assume that in the end we will get what we are waiting for, or we will meet the person with whom we have made an appointment. Sometimes, we enter a waiting room with unknown results and uncertain outcomes. This kind would prove to be the most difficult, faith-building experience of them all. This is the waiting room where you will be challenged beyond your ability to sit and wait. It was in this very place that we, and others we have met along the way, learn to practice Psalm 37:7 which says, "Be still before the Lord and wait patiently for him."

The waiting room of radiation oncology brings to mind one particular young woman whose life deeply touched my soul. Shelley sat in her corner of the room busily putting together reading booklets for her daughter's first grade class. I later learned that this helped keep her mind distracted so she would not focus on her treatment and the reason she was there.

As we chatted with this bubbly, attractive young mother, we learned that her husband (like my own) was also a pilot, giving us a common ground and we felt at ease with one another. I assumed she had breast cancer and was receiving radiation therapy for it. Eventually Shelley's name was called and, to my amazement, I watched my husband get up and walk over to her, shake her hand, and told her it was a pleasure meeting her. This moved me as Jeff is normally a very private person, so this was a little out of character for him. I realized how compassionate my husband's heart was, quietly hidden from anyone on the outside but known to God who sees the inside.

Some moments later, Jeff's name was called and I was left to my thoughts. I suddenly saw Shelley coming around the corner and felt a fluttering in my stomach. "Hug her" is what the Lord seemed to suggest to me, but instead, I held out my hand to her, just like Jeff had done. She grasped it so tightly that when I felt the warmth of her grip, I let my instincts take over and I hugged her. I was surprised by the long, sincere embrace she returned. I told her it was a blessing meeting her today and she remarked, "I was about to say the same to you!" We looked at one another and we saw that we were both Christians.

We briefly exchanged stories. She asked why Jeff was there, and I asked why she was taking radiation treatment. She told me she had an inoperable brain tumor she had been dealing with since 1995. My heart went out to her. I asked if I could pray for her? Right there in the hallway, we bowed our heads and tears rolled down our cheeks. She said she could not believe that God would send her someone to pray for her that day! She was having an emotionally difficult time that day and seemed to need a special touch. So I prayed for her, and now both our faces were wet.

This was truly a holy moment. A divine meeting where lives intersect on the plane of God's will in order to share the broken bread and poured out wine of Christ, so we might be nourished and strengthened and continue walking.

36

Waiting Room Etiquette

Having been through the waiting room experience, I've noticed there are some general, unspoken rules observed by all of us waiters:

Eye contact is not made for at least the first three hours.

Conversation is private, in quiet, hushed tones.

The nervous waiter paces the floor back and forth, off to one side of the room. An invisible boundary line is respectfully drawn around his area. No one enters this space.

The anxious waiter flips through several magazines, never seeing what is on the hundreds of pages turned, only a blurry image of colors and patterns and black typed words.

The patient waiter seems relaxed and calm, looking up as a new waiter enters the room, giving a smile of welcome, but not intrusive.

Seasoned waiters bring a bottle of water, cell phone, a book, and a variety of snacks to accompany them throughout the long day.

Children in the waiting room are a welcome distraction. Their energy, laughter, and oblivion to the serious nature of the waiting room lift the heavy, weighted cloud of anxiety.

After the third hour, a change takes place. Cautious eyes begin to warm with familiarity. A sense of camaraderie enters the atmosphere and guarded conversations become louder, more generalized for others to hear. Entering into another's discussion is acceptable at this point.

By the fifth hour, concern about the other's family member genuinely molds this group together. A sense of gratitude for having each other there permeates the room. We are all grateful for sharing this time with these special people who somehow leave their mark on our lives, in some small, tangible ways. I'll always remember those who offered me their kind words, shared their own stories, or smiled at me quietly as I sat lost in my own thoughts.

37

Lastly But Most Importantly

*I*t is my hope that after reading this book, your heart is comforted by knowing that our God waits with you always. He only needs an invitation. If you need His strength to lean on, He is there for you. He takes over when we allow Him; and He works with us, through us, and in us, through His Word, circumstances, and people. Do you see Him now? He's an amazing God!

Printed in the United States
25944LVS00004B/286-291

9 781597 810012